GARDEN
CREEPY~CRAWLIES

D1391160

GARDEN
CREEPY~CRAWLIES

•MICHAEL CHINERY•

with illustrations by
GUY TROUGHTON

Whittet Books

02011133

Endpaper: Cockchafer beetle, crane-fly and bumble bee.
Title page (clockwise from right): bumble bee, centipede, garden snail, small tortoiseshell butterfly and wasp beetle.

491 416709

First published 1986
Text © 1986 by Michael Chinery
Illustrations © 1986 by Guy Troughton
Whittet Books Ltd, 18 Anley Road, London W14 0BY

Design by Richard Kelly

British Library Cataloguing in Publication Data

Chinery, Michael
    Garden creepy-crawlies.
    1. Insects—Great Britain   2. Gardens—
    Great Britain
    I. Title
    595.70941   QL482.G7
    ISBN 0–905483–44–8

Typeset by Inforum Ltd, Portsmouth
Printed and bound by The Bath Press, Bath

CONTENTS

INTRODUCTION

The garden world

Kneeling in my herbaceous border to deal with a particularly tenacious dock root, I glanced up from ground level to see lupins and delphiniums towering above me like trees. An unusual view of the garden for me, but what, I wondered, would I make of it if I were ant-sized? The border would resemble a forest of skyscrapers. Even the lawn would be a jungle, with the rockery forming a range of mountains and the drive a veritable Sahara. And how would the shed and the garden wall appear? It might all seem rather hostile, but we needn't feel sorry for the ants and the host of other small creatures for whom the garden may be an entire world. They actually like our gardens and thrive on the food and shelter provided. Some like the garden a bit too much and we call them pests, but in general the animal guests do us no harm. In fact, many of them do a lot of good and if you avoid the widespread and indiscriminate use of pesticides, the natural predators, such as the lacewings and ladybirds, will do much of your pest control for you – for free. Your guests will also pollinate the flowers and many of them will give you pleasure at the same time. Butterflies, for example, bring additional colour and, as 'flying flowers', add an extra dimension to the garden.

Although created for our own aesthetic and gastronomic pleasure, the garden clearly has another very important role – that of a nature reserve. Natural habitats are disappearing all around us, but the garden habitat is actually increasing and our gardens can – and must – play a major role in the conservation of wild plants and animals. The garden is really a collection of habitats which, if properly cared for, will ensure the survival of many forms of wildlife without detriment to its other functions. Diversity is the key: the more variety you can provide in the way of habitat and food plants, the more wildlife you will attract and support.

So what are these visitors that we can expect to see in our gardens? The answer depends to some extent on where you live but, being mobile, almost any kind of animal can visit your garden, even if it doesn't actually take up residence. Only recently a friend asked what could be done about the deer that invade his garden and eat his flowers and cabbages. Another actually complained about visiting badgers that dug up his lawn in their search for food – personally I was rather envious and would gladly suffer a damaged lawn for the privilege of watching badgers from my armchair. In the following pages, however, I shall be dealing only with the 'creepy-crawlies' of the garden – small, but immensely fascinating members of the invertebrate world: the world of animals without backbones. Hundreds of different species, belonging to several distinct groups, reside in our gardens, but to the hedgehog and to many gardeners there are just two kinds – crunchy ones and squelchy ones. The crunchies, exemplified by a nice crisp beetle or a woodlouse, are encased in a firm coat or exoskeleton, while the squelchies, represented by the worms and slugs, have no such protection. I have no idea what these creatures taste like, but as far as the hedgehog is concerned it must be akin to choosing between potato crisps and jelly babies. Obviously this division has no scientific basis, for a squelchy grub can turn into a crunchy beetle, and the squelchy slug is clearly related to the crunchy snail – in fact, it is simply a snail without a shell.

In gardening talk, those creepy-crawlies with obvious legs are commonly lumped together as 'insects', with the rest parcelled up as worms, slugs and snails, or simply 'grubs'. Again, this is not a very sound way of looking at things, for most of the 'grubs' turn out to be insects and many of the 'insects' are nothing of the sort. True insects have three pairs of legs when they are mature and most of them also have wings. No other group of invertebrates has wings.

The main groups of garden creepy-crawlies are shown in the accompanying chart and you will find representatives of each group in any garden,

THE MAJOR GROUPS OF GARDEN CREEPY CRAWLIES

ANNELID WORMS, represented in the garden by the earthworms, are legless and their bodies are clearly divided into rings or segments

SLUGS AND SNAILS are molluscs. They have no legs and no segmentation of the body. They glide along on their bellies. Snails have a coiled shell of various shapes into which they can withdraw the whole body, but slugs have little or no shell.

WOODLICE are crustaceans – the only land-living relatives of the crabs. They have seven pairs of legs.

MILLIPEDES are mostly long and slender with many body segments. Most segments have two pairs of legs.

CENTIPEDES are generally flatter than millipedes and often much faster. There is just one pair of legs to each body segment.

Most INSECTS, like this *lacewing*, have two pairs of rather flimsy wings. All have three pairs of legs.

BEETLES and a few other INSECTS have very tough front wings which completely cover the delicate hind wings. Young insects, like the young ladybird on the right, never have proper wings.

Some INSECTS, like this female *bush cricket*, have no wings.

SPIDERS are a large group of ARACHNIDS with a 2-part body.

HARVESTMEN look like spiders but have a one-piece body and make no silk.

MITES are very small ARACHNIDS with a one-piece body and short, spiky legs.

FALSE SCORPIONS are minute ARACHNIDS found mainly in leaf litter.

however small. Many are easy to watch from the comfort of your deck-chair, but you'll soon want to get closer. This book describes some of the fascinating and often amazing dramas played out in your garden, often right under your nose. Find out how the creepy-crawlies feed, mate and defend themselves all around you. And then get out and watch them – on hands and knees if necessary. You'll find a whole new world opening up in your garden. Hopefully, the strong dislike that many people have of insects and other creepy-crawlies will soon evaporate, and you'll find that these small creatures really are worth looking at and worth encouraging into your garden.

Friend or foe?

This is one of the commonest questions asked in the garden, and often the hardest to answer. Some creatures, like the pollinating bees, are clearly beneficial, while many aphids and caterpillars are outright villains down among the flowers and vegetables. But most garden creepy-crawlies are much harder to pigeon-hole: we just don't know enough about their fascinating and often very involved ecology, although it seems likely that the majority of species are on our side or completely neutral. What is certain is that they all have a role to play in the complex web of garden life. Only by watching our garden guests – and enjoying them at the same time – can we unravel their secrets and find out what each one is up to.

If you must label your guests as friends or foes in the manner of the old natural history books, there is a rough and ready rule of thumb to help you deal with the earthbound creepy-crawlies. If a creature creeps or crawls slowly it's unlikely to have to chase food, so it's *probably* a vegetarian and *could* be a pest in the garden. A fast mover, on the other hand, is quite likely to be useful – as a hunter of slower creatures which, as we have just seen, are probably harmful plant-eaters. But this *is* only a rough guide. Consider the predatory centipede: it is certainly useful when eating a harmful slug, but what about when, as often happens, it turns its fangs on another centipede? Is it not then being detrimental to our interests by destroying a useful predator? Remember also that many slow-moving creatures may be harmless or even useful scavengers.

The golden rule should be to ask questions first. Too many people squash first and then ask questions – only to find they've killed unnecessarily – or don't ask questions at all. Spend some time watching your garden guests, and take action only if you witness regular damage to your plants. Even then, fingers are better than poisons.

Pesticides certainly have their place, but don't rush for the aerosol as soon as you find a pest: you might end up doing more damage than the devil himself. The hasty use of chemicals can be like the proverbial sledge-hammer used to crack a nut. Sure, you'll kill lots of greenfly or slugs, but you may also destroy bees and butterflies and possibly birds and hedgehogs and even goldfish in the pond. Once released, there's no knowing where these garden chemicals might end up – perhaps in the dog or cat.

Aphids and caterpillars are easily squashed with your fingers, and no harm is done to the surrounding wildlife. Natural predators, such as ladybirds and lacewings, remain to polish off the pests that you miss. Many other useful allies are described in this book and it is worth bringing some of them into your garden to fight on your behalf. Many hover-fly larvae are greedy aphid-eaters and it is not difficult to acquire an army of them. Marigolds of all kinds – English, French or African – will attract hordes of adult hover-flies to their colourful flowers, and the hover-flies' larvae will deal with aphids on neighbouring plants. So away with convention and start planting a few flowers amongst your vegetables. African and French marigolds (*Tagetes*) have other useful attributes. Their roots exude subst-ances which repel various root-feeding nematode worms – including the notorious potato-root eelworm (see p.24) – and also subdue the growth of such tiresome weeds as couch grass and ground elder. But keep the marigolds away from your cabbages or you might attract rather more cabbage whites than you care to entertain!

NO LEGS:
THE WRIGGLY WORMS

Next time you unearth a large worm in your garden, pick it up and have a good stare at it. You will be looking at what Charles Darwin considered to be the most important animal in the history of the world. Yet one that has only the simplest of brains. So why did Darwin, and Gilbert White before him, lavish so much praise on this blind, legless creature? What makes the wriggling earthworm such a hero?

Drainage engineers

The importance of the earthworm stems from its immense numbers and its tunnelling activities. Numbers vary a great deal according to the nature of the soil, but a well established garden of ¼ acre might well support 25,000 worms. If each worm tunnels just 20 cm (8 inches) per day – probably a very conservative estimate – the upper layers of your soil will be traversed by some 5 km (3 miles) of tunnels. Although these channels soon collapse, they play a major role in draining and aerating the soil. In addition, the continual churning of the soil and the enrichment of the surface layers with the worms' excrement improves its fertility. Gilbert White knew all about this more than 200 years ago and in a letter dated May 20th, 1777, he wrote '. . . worms seem to be the great promoters of vegetation, which would proceed but lamely without them, by boring, perforating, and loosening the soil, and rendering it pervious to rains and the fibres [roots] of plants, by drawing straws and stalks of leaves into it; and, most of all, by throwing up such infinite numbers of lumps of earth, called worm-casts, which, being their excrement, is a fine manure for grain and grass.'

Recent work has shown that earthworms can also benefit our crops via the micro-organisms in the soil. It seems that the alkaline environment produced by the worms' excretions (see p. 18) favours the growth of certain bacteria which secrete vitamin B_{12}, and the latter improves the growth and yield of the crop. The experimental work was carried out with barley, but there seems no reason why our garden plants should not benefit in the same way.

The worm's body

First pick up your worm – it's not nearly as slimy as you might think – and notice that it doesn't have a head. The sharp end is the front. The rear is rather blunt and generally slightly flattened, but if you're in any doubt the worm will soon show you which is the front by thrusting its snout forward. There are no eyes or other obvious sense organs on this front end, but it's extremely sensitive to touch and to chemical stimulation. Some worms have as many as 700 'taste buds' on each square millimetre of the snout. These and other sensory cells are all linked to a collar of nerves just under the surface – the worm's equivalent of a brain. Although there are no eyes, the whole body surface is sensitive to light and the animal always tries to get back into the dark when you uncover it.

Earthworms belong to the large group of animals known as annelids or segmented worms, whose bodies are always composed of numerous rings or segments. You can see these segments very easily in your garden earthworms. There may be as many as 250 in a large worm. Each is a separate fluid-filled compartment, although the gut and other internal organs pass uninterrupted from one segment to the next. On the outside, each segment has four pairs of tiny bristles on its lower surface. You can feel them very easily by stroking the worm's belly from back to front. They serve both as legs and as anchors. Put your worm on a piece of paper and you will hear the bristles scraping the surface as they try to grip it. The worm can move over the paper to some extent, but is quite helpless on a really smooth surface, such as a sheet of glass, which offers no grip at all. Towards the

front end of a mature worm you will see a swollen region known as the clitellum or saddle. Often differing in colour and texture from the rest of the body, it is concerned with reproduction (see p. 21) – hence its appearance only in mature specimens. The exact position of the saddle varies with the species and helps to identify the different kinds of worms. In all our garden species it lies somewhere between the 24th and 44th segments.

What do they eat?

Dead vegetation is the staple diet of earthworms but, with neither teeth nor jaws, the animals can't bite into anything tough. Most of their food consists of small particles which are simply sucked into the mouth, although their mobile lips can nibble small pieces from decaying leaves which have become sufficiently softened. Some species actually live and feed in the layer of dead leaves in woodlands and at the bottoms of hedgerows, and these species can also be found in the garden compost heap. They include the brandling, easily identified by its coat of alternating yellow and dark brown bands.

The boldly marked brandling worm.

The true soil-dwellers, including most of the familiar garden worms, feed largely on decaying roots, but also get a lot of nourishment by sucking in soil and digesting any organic particles in it. Feeding in this way, the worms can eat up to 30 per cent of their own weight in a day. Their chemical senses guide them to areas rich in organic matter, and you will find especially large populations in the soil under the compost heap.

Some soil-dwellers come up to search for dead leaves at the surface on humid nights. Treading carefully, and using a not-too-bright torch, you can watch the worms at work, scouring every spot within reach of their burrows. But it's not all work: for much of the time the worms lie still and just enjoy the fresh air. The hind end remains anchored by the bristles and if the animals are disturbed – by bright lights or heavy footsteps – they shoot back into their holes at high speed. This action is brought about by a chain of extra-large nerve fibres which cause instant contraction of the whole body. When it finds a tasty leaf, the worm grabs it by the stalk or the tip and, holding it largely by suction, drags it into the burrow just as Gilbert White described. Most dead leaves would be cleared from your lawn in this way during the autumn and winter if you didn't sweep them up, but they're not eaten right away. They are left to rot, encouraged by digestive juices smeared on them by the worms, and eaten later. But many are forgotten and their nutrients are returned directly to the soil.

Try pulling it in by the stalk!

Apart from the immediate vicinity of the compost heap, the highest worm population in your garden will undoubtedly be under the lawn, where the animals are virtually undisturbed and well fed by the abundant grass roots and cuttings. The herbaceous garden is also well stocked as a rule, especially if it is regularly manured, but you won't find nearly so many worms in the vegetable plot because the regular cultivations disturb them and also expose them to birds and other enemies. Sandy soils have the lowest worm populations of all, because they dry out quickly and also because they are rather acidic and few worm species can tolerate high acidity.

Garbage guzzlers in the home

Many American homes boast a worm-bin or, if you prefer long names, a vermicomposting system. The idea is that you employ worms, installed in a suitable container, to nibble their way through your kitchen and table scraps, and you then use the resulting compost for your house plants. It's also recommended as a way of breeding worms for fishing. The worms used are not ordinary garden earthworms, but the litter-feeding species such as the brandling and various small red worms that can be found in your compost heap. It all sounds a bit smelly, but fans of the system assure us that it is not and that a thriving worm bin can masquerade as a bench seat in even the best of sitting rooms. It's an admirable idea for recycling vegetable waste, and it obviously can be fun, but you need plenty of space. If you produce about a pound (half a kilo) of garbage each day – an under-estimate for most families using fresh vegetables – you will need a bin with a surface area of about 6 sq. ft (·55 sq. m.). It should be no more than about a foot deep, and when it is full it must be left for several months for the worms to complete their work. This means another bin, and more space, if you wish to carry on composting; and another 2 lb (·9 kilos) of worms – the recommended amount to deal with a daily ration of a pound of garbage. If you produce too much compost for your house plants you can always spread some on the garden – but if you have a garden why not make your compost there in the usual way?

How do they move?

Earthworms rely for movement on their bristles, two powerful sets of muscles, and the fact that the water-filled body compartments cannot be compressed. Reducing the process to basics, we can say that the worm anchors its rear end in the ground by digging its bristles into the tunnel walls and then pushes the front end forward by a combination of muscular and hydraulic action. Contraction of circular muscles in the front end causes the segments to become thinner, and because the fluid in them cannot be

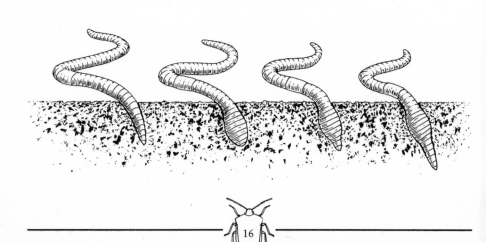

compressed, these segments become longer. The front part of the body thus surges forward. Muscles running along the body relax and become stretched at this stage of the process. The worm then anchors its front end and, by contracting the longitudinal muscles, it draws the back end forward – as long as it remembers to release the bristles at the rear. In fact, the process is more complex than I have described, because several sections are on the move at any one time, with anchored sections between them, but the principle remains the same.

You have only to hold a worm in a clenched fist to discover the amazing power of its hydraulic system. It will probe between your fingers in a determined effort to escape. The power of the muscles and the grip of the bristles are also well demonstrated if you try to pull a worm from its burrow, and you can see why birds have such a job to haul worms from the ground.

It's the early bird . . .

Tunnels and worm-casts

The earthworm creates its tunnel system partly by forcing its body between the soil particles, using the hydraulic power just described, and partly by eating its way through the soil – rather like a modern tunnelling machine that gulps in rock at one end and spews it out at the other. But the worm has no teeth to chew through the soil and it merely sucks in small particles that it has loosened with its snout. It digests the organic material in the soil and passes the mineral matter out at the hind end. The tunnel picks up a lining of slime from the worm's body, and some species plaster the walls with their excrement, giving the tunnel some degree of stability. The worms are quite happy to save energy by moving along pre-existing tunnels on occasion, but even the reinforced tunnels do not last very long and the soil is continually being re-worked. One of Darwin's more astonishing, but undoubtedly accurate, conclusions was that every particle of top-soil had passed through a worm on many occasions and would do so many more times.

The worm-casts that appear on our lawns and, less conspicuously, elsewhere in our gardens are the worms' droppings and they seem to offend an awful lot of gardeners. Brush them from your lawn by all means if they worry you, but scatter them elsewhere in your garden or else let them dry and crumble and then put them back on the lawn, for they contain valuable plant foods. The worst thing you can do is to use a worm-killer. It will get rid of the worms and their casts, but it will also get rid of the aeration and drainage channels under your lawn. Which do you prefer – a few worm casts or a soggy, moss-infested patch of grass? If you're so finicky that you can't stand any casts on the lawn, try a surface dressing of ammonium sulphate. This will discourage those species that cast at the surface (see p. 19) without harming the others and impairing their drainage work. The dressing will also act as a fertilizer for your grass.

Darwin, who wrote a long book on his observations of worms and their effect on the soil, estimated that about 16,000 kg (35,000 lb) of worm-casts

Going down?

were scattered over an acre of pastureland every year – amounting to a depth of about 5 mm (¹/₅ inch) if spread evenly over the surface. As most of this material is mined from deeper levels, stones and other objects on the surface gradually sink. Dig into an old lawn and you will find the upper layers virtually stone-free. As the worms cannot swallow anything more than about 2 mm in diameter, the soil that they bring to the surface is also extremely fine and of an ideal texture for the growth of plants.

Only two of our British earthworms – *Allolobophora nocturna* and *A. longa* – regularly make casts on the surface. The rest do their business in the upper parts of their tunnels, but the effect on the soil is just the same.

The ploughing action of the worms counteracts the action of rainfall, which gradually washes minerals down from the surface layers and away from the plant roots that need them. By swallowing soil in the lower layers and bringing it back to the surface in the form of worm-casts, the worms make the minerals available to the plants again. The breakdown of organic materials as they pass through the worms also releases valuable minerals for the plants.

How deep do they go?

The majority of earthworm activity takes place in the top 25 cm (10 inches) of the soil, and some species never even get to this depth. Our larger species,

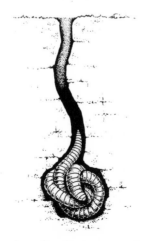

Allolobophora goes to sleep for the summer tightly coiled in a chamber deep in the soil.

however, including the two *Allolobophora* species and *Lumbricus terrestris*, regularly go down to depths of about a metre (a yard). In really cold or dry weather they may dive even deeper. Deep digging during the summer – when lifting early potatoes, for example – may bring up a number of tightly coiled worms which show little inclination to uncoil and crawl away. These will be the two *Allolobophora* species already mentioned, which habitually go into a summer sleep known as aestivation. As these are the two worms that produce surface casts, you will not normally find casts during the summer months, although they may be abundant from October to May – as long as the weather is not too cold. Breathing at depth presents the worms with no great problems because the animals breathe through their skins. A dense network of blood vessels lies just under the surface and absorbs oxygen from the air spaces in the soil, aided by the red blood pigment haemoglobin. This pigment, which we have in our own blood, has a great liking for oxygen and it can absorb enough for the worms' needs even if the amounts in the soil are rather low.

Each-way sex

An earthworm is normally male and female at the same time. Biologists term it 'hermaphrodite'. But it can't normally serve itself and it must find a partner. This arrangement might seem a little odd, but it is really of great value to slow-moving creatures that don't bump into too many of their neighbours. It means that *any* adult of the same species is a potential mate, so the chances of finding a suitable partner are much improved. Most species mate in their tunnels, but *Lumbricus terrestris* is less shy about its sex life and commonly copulates on the surface in full view of anyone who wants to watch. You can see the animals at it at almost any time of the year, although damp nights in early summer are best and you won't see any

Locked in a slimy embrace, two earthworms exchange sperm on the surface.

activity in frosty weather. Use a dim torch or one covered with red plastic to avoid disturbing the worms.

Sex-seeking worms stretch out from their burrows just like those that are searching for leaves, and they meet up with their neighbours through scent and perhaps through minute vibrations. Compatibility established, the worms twist their bodies so that their bellies come together, but pointing in opposite directions and still maintaining contact with their own burrows. Their bristles dig into each other in a stimulating embrace and their bodies become wrapped in a corset of mucus which keeps them close together, sometimes for hours. Each worm receives sperm from the other, and then they separate. The saddle then plays its part by secreting a detachable collar of mucus. The worm wriggles backwards out of this collar, squirting into it a number of eggs and a delivery of the other worm's sperm, which has been stored until now in special pouches. When free of the body, the ends of the collar seal themselves up to form a little spherical cocoon in which the eggs mature, although very often only one egg comes to fruition in each cocoon. Several cocoons may be produced from one pairing. The eggs hatch after several or many weeks and the larger species may take as long as 18 months to reach maturity. Those that escape their numerous enemies may live for ten years or more.

The earthworm's enemies

Hedgehogs and shrews are the main worm-eating mammals in the garden, snapping them up in the hedge bottom and also taking many of the less wary individuals feeding or mating on the surface at night. Moles are even greater enemies of the earthworms, although they are not usually very important in the garden. They catch almost all their worms under the ground and your average mole probably needs about 25 good sized worms or their equivalent each day. It often catches more than this and stores the surplus in underground larders after chewing or biting off the front ends. Surprisingly, this drastic treatment does not necessarily kill the worms. Many of them regenerate the lost or damaged segments and, if the mole doesn't return for them, they can eventually wander away. Rear ends are even more easily regenerated, but worms that are cut near the middle – as often happens when the gardener is busy with the spade – usually die: contrary to popular belief, the saddle is not a scar showing where a worm has grown together again. Regeneration of lost parts is less common among the smaller species that live in leaf litter.

A shrew struggles with a wriggling earthworm.

Birds are also major predators of earthworms, with blackbirds, thrushes and starlings competing for them on the lawn. Watch how the birds stalk over the grass and cock their heads from side to side as they listen and look for the slightest movements that might indicate a worm just under the surface. And watch the ensuing tug-of-war as the bird strains to overcome the resistance of the worm's bristles and haul its prize from the ground. You can see these battles mainly during the first half of the year, when the ground is fairly moist and the worms are near the surface. During the autumn, when there is plenty of fruit and other food about, the birds don't bother to wrestle with worms very much.

Naming earthworms

For practical purposes, earthworms are earthworms and the gardener need not concern himself with naming the different species. In fact, about ten different kinds are commonly turned up in the garden, but only an experienced 'wormologist' will be able to identify them all, and even then a microscope will often be necessary. Accurate identification involves measuring the distances between the bristles as well as counting the number of segments. If you can't recognize a species and distinguish it from its friends you can't give it a name of its own, so it's not surprising that only one of our earthworms has received a common name: the brandling, which is easily identified by its banded coat. The rest must soldier on with long scientific names, given and used only by the boffins. Common garden species include *Lumbricus terrestris* – our largest species – *L. rubellus, L. castaneus, Allolobophora longa* and *A. nocturna*. The following table will help you to recognize them.

Name	Colour	No. of Segments	Position of Saddle*	Total length
Lumbricus terrestris	Brown-red to violet, with orange-red saddle	110–160	(31) 32–37	90–300mm (3½–12 in)
L. rubellus	Reddish brown or violet; iridescent above	95–120	(26) 27–31 (32) (much broader than neighbouring segments)	60–150mm (2½–6 in)
L. castaneus	Chestnut or violet brown with orange saddle	82–100	28–33	30–35mm (1¹/₅–1²/₅ in)
Allolobophora longa	Grey; iridescent	160–200	(27) 28–35	90–120mm (3½–¾ in)
A. nocturna	Reddish brown with paler saddle	200–250	(27) 28–35	90–180mm (3½–7 in)

* Figures indicate the segments normally covered by the saddle, with (in brackets) the other segments sometimes involved.

The thunderworms

Thunderworms are easily mistaken for bits of cream or brown cotton draped over low-growing plants – until they start to move and weave intricate patterns with their long, slender bodies. Up to 50 cm (20 inches) long, and little thicker than sewing cotton, they literally tie themselves in knots as they twine around the vegetation – although they can untie themselves just as easily. These strange worms, which are not uncommon in the garden, get their name because they are most often seen after heavy rain in the summer. You can also find them coiled up amongst the roots of plants in drier weather, although they are then much more difficult to see. A lens will show you that their bodies are not made up of segments like the earthworm body, and the animals belong to a totally different group – the nematodes or roundworms. They spend their early lives as parasites inside the bodies of various insects, boring their way out when mature to finish their days living freely in the soil. Mating takes place here, or during excursions over soggy vegetation, and the female lays her eggs in the ground. The young worms readily find their way into their insect hosts. There are many other kinds of nematode worms, most of them of microscopic size. The majority live freely in the soil, feeding on decaying plant and animal matter, but others, known as eelworms, attack roots. The potato root eelworm causes severe losses to potato crops by burrowing into the fine roots and weakening the plants.

The thunderworm tying up clover leaves.

NO LEGS:
THE SLUGS AND SNAILS

Devoid of any kind of leg, slugs and snails have developed an efficient, if rather slow, method of creeping around on their bellies. Watched from above, they move without visible means of propulsion, but the mystery is readily solved if you put one of these creatures in a jam jar or on a sheet of glass and watch from below. Slime or mucus pours out from glands on the underside and the animal virtually swims along this lubricated track. Muscular waves ripple forward along the belly, lifting each part in turn and wafting the whole body smoothly forward on the mucus. The waves take the form of alternating light and dark bands, of which only the dark areas are raised and actually moving forward. The light bands are stationary and

firmly pressed against the sticky mucus. As well as lubricating the animal's passage and protecting the soft tissues from sharp objects, the mucus serves as an adhesive and is quite strong enough to hold the animal when it decides to go mountaineering on the garden wall or on your window panes. The slime remains behind and dries as a shiny trail to show where the animal has been.

Slugs and snails belong to the huge group of soft-bodied animals known as molluscs, and within this group they form the class of about 60,000 species known as gastropods – a name meaning belly-foot and describing the animals perfectly. The muscular gliding organ is called the foot rather than the belly, and its lower surface is the sole. The great majority of gastropods live in water, but there are still plenty of terrestrial species, including about 80 kinds of snail and 20 kinds of slug living in the British Isles. Although several can survive prolonged drought, activity reaches its peak in damp conditions because the body loses moisture very easily and the production of the vital mucus also requires a good deal of water.

Take a torch into the garden on a damp summer night for the best views of slugs and snails in action, crawling all over the vegetation and also exploring your walls and paths. But don't go hunting for them outside the garden unless you can cope with comment and opinion – often exceedingly impolite – when the pubs turn out. You will also need a plausible explanation if the law turns up. I once had some difficulty in convincing a policeman that I was exploring a roadside ditch in the middle of the night in order to find some slugs for an artist to paint.

You'll probably crunch a few snails noisily under foot as you walk around your garden; return to the corpses later and look for beetles and centipedes enjoying the feast. Snails are busy in the garden even in heavy rain, but slugs, with no shelly umbrellas to protect them, are less keen on the rain and usually stay under cover until it stops.

By day slugs and snails generally tuck themselves away in secluded spots, although they may come out to feed after a shower. Snails often use the same resting places day after day, as you can easily prove by marking a few shells with paint or a wax crayon. Unused flower-pots are favourites with snails, which glue themselves firmly to the inner walls to reduce water loss. Piles of logs and stones are also used as sleeping quarters, as are clumps of low-growing plants like pinks and aubretia. Slugs also have 'homes', although it is less easy to discover this by marking. Slugs lack the protection afforded by the shell of the snail, but there are compensations: the slug can squeeze its soft and flexible body into very small spaces under loose bark and even between paving slabs on the path. Such places generally provide adequate protection, but squeezing into small holes can sometimes be dangerous, as some slugs discover when they seek shelter inside electrical fittings – a truly shocking experience!

In really dry weather the animals don't even come out at night for fear of desiccation. They die rapidly if they try to roam about in unsaturated air, and so in really dry conditions the sensible snail retires into its shell and seals the entrance with a layer of mucus. The latter hardens into a waterproof front door, known as the epiphragm, which keeps the snail snug and moist until better conditions return. The animal can survive in this inactive state for several months. Snails shut up shop in just the same way in very cold weather, often gluing themselves together in great masses. In southern Europe, where the ground gets extremely hot in the summer, many kinds of snails actually climb up the vegetation before settling down to sleep – or aestivate if you want the technical term. They may be fully exposed to the sun for several hours each day, but their pale shells reflect a lot of the heat and the animals stay several degrees cooler than they would on the ground – where they might literally be cooked.

Slugs dislike dry weather even more than the snails and generally burrow into the ground in dry conditions. Even in saturated air they lose a lot of water in mucus production, and experiments have shown that when they have lost about $1/6$th of their body weight they slow down and seek shelter. When sitting still, they soon regain the lost moisture by absorbing water from the air, and then they're off on their travels again. Under experimental conditions, various slugs have recovered after losing more than half of their body weight, but in nature they would have burrowed into the soil long before reaching such a critical state. By comparison, humans need hospital treatment after losing water equivalent to only a tenth of their body weight. Even camels cannot recover from the loss of about a third of their body weight.

The shell

The snail's shell is secreted by the animal itself and the snail can never leave its shell. It does not moult and grow a new one like the arthropods (see p. 42). New material is continually added at the rim of the shell and growth lines are usually clearly visible, running across the whorls and parallel to the lip. Growth may stop altogether during the winter, and also during prolonged summer drought, and these periods are often marked by irregular seams where later growth does not tie in neatly with the older material.

The shell is produced by the mantle – a thick cloak of skin enveloping that part of the body permanently inside the shell. Gently lift up an active snail and you will see the edge of the mantle forming a collar around the body close to the mouth of the shell. A small hole may open and close on the right hand edge of the mantle. This is the breathing pore, leading to the mantle cavity or lung between the mantle and the body. Aggravate your snail and it will retract into its shell, appearing to swallow the foot into the lips of the mantle. The latter then becomes quite conspicuous until it is buried in a mass of protective froth. The edge of the mantle secretes most of the shell. It produces the thin, outer layer of the shell first, and if you look at young snails, especially in spring and early summer, you will often find that the rim of the shell has only this soft, horny layer. The inner, chalky layers are laid down a little later. Snails can make limited repairs to the inner layer after damage, but the horny layer, which gives the shell most of its colour, cannot be replaced. On reaching maturity, the adult snail strengthens the rim of the shell with a swollen lip or a ridge just inside the rim and no further growth takes place.

All our land snails produce spirally coiled shells, but there is still plenty of variation – from almost flat, through the typical top-shape, to the skittle-shaped shells of the *Clausilia* species that we find among the mosses on our garden walls. The shape of the shell and the number of whorls are particularly important in identifying snails – usually more useful than colour, which often fades or disappears completely from older shells as the horny layer wears away. Height and breadth are obviously important, but remember that these measurements, as do the number of whorls, increase as the snail gets older.

If you peer underneath the shell you may see a small hole – the umbilicus – passing up the centre of the spire. The relative width of this hole may help to identify the snail, but it is not always present: in many species it is

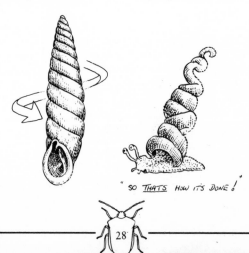

" SO *THATS* HOW IT'S DONE! "

obliterated in the adult by the broad inner lip. The direction of coiling is virtually constant for each species and the great majority of shells are right-handed: hold the shell upright in front of you and you will see that the opening is almost always on the right of the spire. Among the few species that are habitually left-handed or sinistral are the *Clausilia* species mentioned above.

A fair amount of calcium is obviously necessary for shell formation and you will find a greater variety of snails on lime-rich soils than elsewhere. The shells are also thicker – sometimes so thick that they are difficult to break. But on lime-deficient soils the same species may have much thinner and more brittle shells. Several species are in the process of evolving thinner or smaller shells, enabling them to flourish on all kinds of soils. And if this trend continues to its logical conclusion we end up with – slugs!

Slugs – snails without shells

Slugs are merely snails that have lost their shells during their evolution. The digestive and reproductive organs, which are contained in the snail's hump and neatly packed into the shell, have been repacked into the slug's more streamlined body, but otherwise almost everything remains the same. The mantle is smaller, but still there – perched on the back like a short cape and still enclosing the lung. Look for the breathing pore on the right-hand edge of the mantle.

Three families of slug occur in Europe, exhibiting rather different internal structures and undoubtedly descended from different groups of snails. The slugs are thus not a close-knit group and their families are no more closely related to each other than to the various snail families.

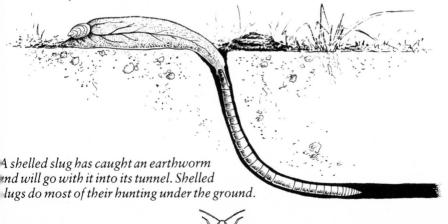

A shelled slug has caught an earthworm and will go with it into its tunnel. Shelled slugs do most of their hunting under the ground.

Although I have said that the slugs have lost their shells, this is not absolutely true. The round-backed slugs (family Arionidae) and the keeled slugs (Limacidae) have a small internal shell, although it is often no more than a few chalky granules hidden under the mantle, while the shelled slugs (Testacellidae) still have a tiny external shell perched on the tail end like a hooked fingernail. These shelled slugs, of which only three species live in Britain, are rarely seen because they spend much of their time chasing worms in the soil. The tapering body is well suited for this mode of life and the slugs can squeeze themselves into the worms' tunnels. On meeting a worm, the tongue (see p. 31) is shot out to impale it. Extra long teeth on the tongue hold the worm firmly and it is then slowly sucked into the mouth like a piece of spaghetti.

Eyes on stalks

Our slugs and most of our land-living snails have two pairs of tentacles on the head, with the eyes at the tips of the longer pair. Snails' eyes are generally larger than those of the slugs, with more light-sensitive cells behind the lens, but they are never very efficient organs and it is unlikely that any of the animals ever forms a real picture of anything. The main function of the eyes is to distinguish light from dark, and they do this very well. The animals are attracted towards dim light at night, and this gets them out into the open to feed. Snails surrounded by blocks of wood – veritable sky-scrapers to the snails – make unerringly for the gaps between the blocks at night, indicating that they really do react to light and dark: they do not bump into the blocks before finding their way between them. Similarly, a snail will turn away if you put your hand in front of it at night. The general body surface also has some sensitivity to light. The tentacles pick up smells which lead the animals towards food. Most of the smelling organs are on the smaller pair of tentacles, where they mingle with 'taste buds' as well, but there are some on the longer tentacles and experiments have indicated that these are primarily long-distance receptors. Removal of the longer tentacles meant that the animals could find food only when it was within about 20 cm (8 inches), but complete animals homed in on food from more than 50 cm (20 inches). Incidentally, slugs and snails have good powers of regeneration and are able to replace lost tentacles within a few weeks, so removing them is not so cruel as it sounds.

If you have ever handled slugs or snails, you will know that the tentacles are extremely sensitive to touch and are withdrawn at the slightest provoca

ion – good protection against accidental damage. Withdrawal involves
pulling the tentacle outside-in, rather as you might pull in the finger of a
glove, with the aid of a muscle running the whole length of the tentacle.
Extension, which you can witness very easily by putting a snail down after
aggravating it, is brought about by pumping blood into the tentacle.

Sandpaper tongues

Our garden slugs and snails feed on a wide assortment of materials. Some
are purely carnivorous (see p. 30), but the majority are omnivorous
scavengers feeding on fungi, decaying plant matter, carrion, and even
animal dung. Relatively few species care for 'greens', but those that do like
greenstuff are all too common in the garden and they make themselves very
unpopular with gardeners by destroying seedlings and other tender plants.
Several species are partial to grass cuttings in the early stages of decay: you
sometimes see them in their hundreds on recently mown verges, especially
after rain. The animals find and test food with their sensitive lips as well as
with their tentacles.

Slugs and snails have no real jaws and they feed by rasping their food with
a ribbon-like tongue called the radula. This is a very distinctive organ,
possessed by no other group of animals, and it can deal equally well with
both hard and soft materials. Covered with thousands of minute, horny
teeth, the radula is just like a tiny strip of sandpaper and a few licks can

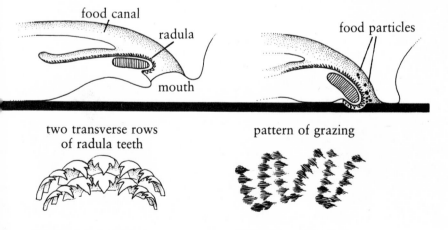

two transverse rows
of radula teeth

pattern of grazing

The radula is thrust out of the mouth to rasp away at the food.

reduce a leaf to shreds. Much of the action is just like that of a rasp or a piece
of sandpaper, but there is also a hint of the circular saw, especially at the end
of each lick when the radula curves back into the mouth. The teeth swing
into a more erect position at this moment and tend to rip through the food.
You can watch the radula at work by giving a slug or a snail a piece of
lettuce and watching from below. Assuming the animal is hungry, holes will
soon appear in the leaf and, with the aid of a lens, you can see the toothy
radula working its way around the edges of the holes. You can even hear it if
the lettuce is nice and crisp.

The radula can also be used to rasp encrusting algae from various
surfaces, and if your greenhouse is a bit too green you might persuade a few
slugs and snails to clean it for you. This isn't a recommended method of
greenhouse cleaning, but it does give you another opportunity to see the
radula at work. And you can also see the tooth patterns – clear areas caused
by the passage of the tooth rows through the algae. Each species has its own
tooth pattern. You can turn your old over-exposed photographic negatives
into research tools in this field. Soak them thoroughly and put them in a box
with a few slugs and snails: the animals will leave their radular patterns as
they rasp their way through the soft emulsion. But you will need a lens to see
the differences; or you could mount the negatives and enlarge them with a
slide projector.

Just like sandpaper, the radula becomes worn with use and the tip
crumbles away – usually to be swallowed with the food. But the animals
don't starve. The radula is a continuously growing strip, rather like our own
fingernails, and the animals are never without teeth. New rows of teeth are
always pushing forward to replace those lost from the tip.

When love is in the air

Our slugs and all but very few of our terrestrial snails are hermaphroditic
creatures with male and female organs in the same individual, just as we
saw in the earthworms. Some species go in for do-it-yourself and, in the
absence of a partner, they can fertilize themselves quite efficiently, but
cross-fertilization is more fun, and the preferred practice; each individual
then lays eggs after mating. Elaborate courtship behaviour generally pre
cedes mating, and the peeping tom with a torch may witness some really
fascinating displays.

None is stranger than the courtship of the great grey slug (*Lima.
maximus*), which is not uncommon around the garden compost heap. The

performance begins soon after dark on summer nights, with the first act taking place on the ground as the two animals get to know each other. They crawl around in a circle, often nose to tail, and secrete large amounts of mucus. This foreplay is said to go on for up to an hour, but in my own experience the slugs can't hold out that long. One inconsiderate pair were in such a hurry that they were into the second act before I could set up my camera – less than five minutes after they first met. The second act begins when one of the slugs makes for a vertical surface, such as a wall or a tree trunk, and starts to climb. The other responds eagerly to this molluscan equivalent of 'come up and see my etchings' and follows right behind. On reaching a mutually acceptable spot, the two animals go into a clinch, exploring each other intently with their tentacles and gradually becoming more and more entwined. They exude a very sticky mucus and, as they continue to coil around each other, the mucus forms a sturdy rope. The slugs gradually lower themselves at the end of this rope and mating finally takes place in mid-air, as much as a metre below the support.

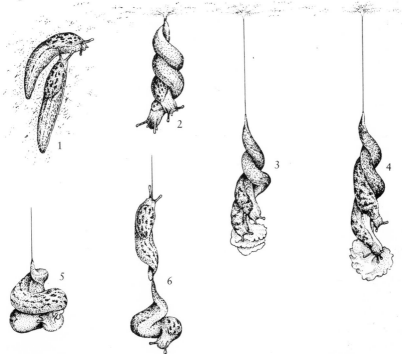

Stages in the nuptials of the great grey slug. The fan-shaped genitalia are clearly seen in stage 4.

Act three starts with the gelatinous, white genitalia oozing out from the front of each slug and becoming fan-shaped. Sperm transfer takes place with the genitalia closely entwined and at this stage, with so much equipment on external view, the slugs' bodies look quite shrivelled. Then, quite suddenly, the genitalia are disengaged and withdrawn into the bodies. After a final embrace, with their bodies forming a tight ball, the slugs separate. One usually climbs back up the rope, but the other has options: it may climb up, often eating the mucus as it goes, or it may extend the rope and lower itself to the ground. The aerial part of the performance generally takes between 30 and 60 minutes, although it sometimes goes on well into the night. Pearly white eggs are laid by both slugs within a few weeks, usually in small batches hidden in the soil or the compost heap or tucked under logs and stones. Some eggs hatch within a week or two, but others in the same batch may delay hatching for several weeks, or even months. This happens with most slugs and reduces the risk of a whole family being wiped out by unfavourable conditions.

Most other slugs mate on or under the ground, having become acquainted by following each other's slime trails. They often eat the mucus and it seems likely that, at least in some species, receptive animals doctor their own slime trails with an aphrodisiac that excites their suitors. The slugs circle around each other in a puddle of mucus and eventually copulate by poking out their genitals – less impressive than those of the great grey slug – and exchanging sperm. As well as egging on the partners, the mucus undoubtedly provides some degree of protection against hungry hedgehogs and other enemies which would otherwise quickly put an end to the nuptials by gobbling up the participants. It can't be much fun to get a mouthful of sticky mucus – it's bad enough getting it on your fingers. The aerial antics of the great grey slug also probably evolved as a way of avoiding disturbance by predators.

Love-darts

Snails will mate wherever they meet, although they usually manage to find some privacy amongst the vegetation. As with slugs, there is a certain amount of pre-nuptial smearing with mucus as the animals get acquainted, and then, as they lie with their right sides snuggling up to each other, their genitals are poked out and mutual copulation takes place. The animals spend some hours in this condition and, although mating is primarily a nocturnal pursuit, it is not uncommon to find them still locked in their embrace in the morning. Examine such a pair of garden snails (*Helix aspersa*) or banded snails (see p. 38) and you might well see a chalky dart sticking into the flesh of one or both animals. These darts are fired by each snail into the body of its partner as the ultimate aphrodisiac to trigger off the final stages of mating. Only the more advanced snails possess such equipment, and the darts don't always go in far enough to stay put. The exact shape of the dart varies with the species and helps to distinguish closely related types, such as the two banded snails.

Although slugs and snails are hermaphrodites, mutual exchange of sperm does not always occur. One individual may take on a female role and accept sperm from its partner without giving any in return. These roles are not permanent, however, and may well be reversed at the next mating – which, in some of the smaller species, may take place almost immediately, with several affairs in a single night.

Slayers of slugs and snails

Despite their protective shells, snails have many enemies in the garden. The most familiar is undoubtedly the song thrush, which has a unique method of extracting the soft flesh. Snails are sought in the herbage and brought to a favourite execution block known as the anvil. This is usually a prominent stone, often on a rockery, or the bird may simply choose a small area of concrete path. It is usually some distance from the nest during the breeding season, thus avoiding drawing attention to the nest site, while at other times the bird may not actually have a regular anvil – any convenient stone will do. Gripping the lip of the shell in its beak, the thrush brings it down hard on the anvil. Several attempts may be needed to crack the shell sufficiently for the body to be hauled out, and this produces the regular and surprisingly

loud tapping sound that you hear in the garden. After extracting the body
the thrush wipes it on the ground to remove most of the mucus and ther
swallows it. Garden snails and banded snails are the main victims, as you
can see from the numerous shell fragments left lying around the anvil
Youngsters sometimes accompany their mothers to the dining table, to be
fed and also probably to learn a thing or two about snail-bashing. Snails are
eaten at any time of year, but most commonly during the spring and early
summer.

Blackbirds and mistle thrushes also eat plenty of snails, but they haven'
discovered the anvil technique and they break the shells as best they car
with their beaks. Small shells are simply crushed and swallowed. Hedge
hogs, frogs, toads and slow worms enjoy a few snails as well, generally
taking the smaller and thinner shelled species. If your garden is in rura
surroundings with plenty of grassland you might even find the glow worm
attacking your snails. Look for a woodlouse-shaped creature half concealed
in the shell as it tucks into the juicy flesh. This is the larval glow worm
which produces just a faint greenish glow at its hind end.

Slugs are, as one might expect, eaten by much the same animals as snails
but the lack of a protective shell makes them even more vulnerable
Hedgehogs, for example, eat far more slugs than snails, and the same is true
of shrews, frogs and toads. Slow worms, which are not uncommon in the
damper and grassier gardens, account for huge numbers of slugs, including
quite large ones. Ground beetles and rove beetles, such as the devil'
coach-horse (see p. 89) also eat plenty of slugs. But don't think that the slug
are entirely without protection: their mucus is a deterrent to some animals

SOME SNAILS AND SLUGS OF THE GARDEN

GARDEN SNAIL

One of the worst pests and familiar to all gardeners, it is not at all fussy what it eats. With its healthy appetite, it will reduce a freshly planted cabbage to a leafless stump in a couple of hours.

STRAWBERRY SNAIL

As common as the garden snail, but slightly less damaging because it is smaller. It swarms over low vegetation on damp evenings and is not particularly associated with strawberries. The mature shell has a strong white ridge just inside the lip.

GARLIC GLASS SNAIL

An abundant scavenger in the compost heap, and also found under logs and stones. It gives off a strong smell of garlic when handled.

GARDEN SLUG

Almost as damaging as the netted slug, this pest causes severe damage to strawberries, turnips and potatoes. It has no keel and produces orange mucus.

SOWERBY'S SLUG

Very similar to the last species in looks and habits, but distinguished by its yellow mucus and plain white sole.

NETTED SLUG

Public enemy number one among the slugs, being abundant and ready to attack a wide range of plants. It commonly lurks in the middle of lettuces. Its normal mucus is colourless, but when disturbed it pumps out a thick white slime. It has a short keel or ridge on the hind end.

BUDAPEST SLUG

Largely subterranean in habit and particularly damaging to potatoes and root crops. Distinguished from the next species by its colourless mucus and by the dark central stripe along the sole.

YELLOW SLUG

Rarely found away from human habitation, it enjoys life in cellars and out-houses where it feeds largely on moulds and rotting matter – anything except green plants, so you can welcome this animal without qualms. The great grey slug (see p. 32) has a similar diet, although it will occasionally nibble a tender plant.

LARGE BLACK SLUG

Abundant on roadside verges after rain, it often wanders into gardens and, if it can't find enough rotting vegetation, it may munch a few young plants by night. It has no keel. Adults may be black, brick-red, orange, or even yellowish grey, with the lighter forms more common in the south. Youngsters are always pale. When disturbed, this slug contracts to a prune-like hemisphere and rocks from side to side to deter would-be predators.

especially birds, and in some species it is extremely sticky. Molest a large black slug (see p. 37) and you will soon discover how sticky it is – quite tacky enough to gum up the works of a bird's beak. Those birds, such as thrushes and blackbirds, that do eat slugs concentrate on the smaller species but are still careful to wipe most of the mucus off on the ground before swallowing the animals.

Varied patterns

If your garden is surrounded by hedges or grassy habitats it will probably support a number of snails with brown bands running around their shells. There may be up to five bands on each whorl, although some snails have no bands at all. The ground colour of the shells ranges from pale yellow through pink, to dark brown – although most garden specimens are yellow. There are actually two species involved, commonly known as the white-lipped and the brown-lipped banded snails. The former usually has a white lip to the shell when mature, while its cousin has a brown lip, but this is not an infallible guide and it does not work, of course, with immature specimens. The surest way of distinguishing the two species is to examine the mating darts, but this is not something that you can do as you wander round your garden. Unless the darts have been released during mating, you will have to dissect the snails!

White-lipped snail.

Brown-lipped snail.

These two banded snails have generated an enormous amount of research, aimed at finding out why they are so variable and how the variations are maintained from year to year. It's a complex story, but it is clear that predation by birds plays a big role by removing snails that are unsuited to their habitats. Most hedgerow and garden snails are distinctly banded, for this provides the best camouflage in the 'broken' vegetation of these habitats.

Control them

Some degree of control is necessary, especially, on damper soils, if you want to keep slug and snail damage in your garden to a minimum, but this does not necessitate widespread use of poisons. I admit to using small quantities of slug pellets – containing metaldehyde – to protect choice rockery bulbs and susceptible bedding plants such as French marigolds, but where possible I prefer other methods. A little untidiness is not a bad thing here, for many of the marauding molluscs are just as happy or even happier with dead leaves than with growing plants: so don't trim all the outer leaves from your lettuces. Another old trick is to surround your prize plants with cinders: although the slugs and snails lubricate their paths very efficiently, they seem to dislike crossing the ring of cinders. Old planks or pieces of sacking laid in slug-infested areas will attract lots of the pests by providing tempting daytime retreats, and you can then do what you will with the slugs. Personally, I scatter them on a nearby grass verge. Searching by torchlight is another way of collecting slugs and snails from your plants – time-consuming, but a good way of finding out just what conditions bring

CINDERS...?
WELL YOU'RE NOT
GOING TO THE BALL

them out. If you must use poisons, try to cover the pellets with wire netting to keep out birds and hedgehogs, and remove all dead slugs and snails each morning; you might be denying the birds and hedgehogs some of their natural food, but at least you won't be poisoning them and they can continue to do their bit towards your garden pest control. If you're bothered by snails and have no concrete paths in the garden it's worth scattering a few large stones here and there – somewhere for the thrushes to bash the snails on. The birds won't carry the snails very far, and if you have no suitable anvils in your garden they will do their hunting elsewhere. A safer way of destroying slugs is to use the time-honoured beer-trap to send them merrily on their way. A dish of beer will attract and drown a surprisingly large number of slugs in a night.

Snails for dinner

Posh restaurants often have escargots on the menu. They may sound better than snails, but that's what they are. They generally turn out to be Roman snails (Helix pomatia), the largest of our British snails, with a pale brown or cream shell up to 50 mm (2 inches) in diameter. It was once thought that these large snails were brought to Britain by the Romans, who used to keep them in special enclosures and fatten them for the table – allegedly feeding them on bran soaked with wine – but the discovery of sub-fossil shells has proved that the Roman snail was living in Britain long before the Romans arrived. It is not uncommon on chalk and limestone in southern England.

But even the 'ordinary' garden snail (Helix aspersa) is edible and it was once the subject of snail-hunting festivals in some rural areas. It is still prized as a delicacy in France and other parts of Europe, where youngsters can easily augment their pocket money by collecting a few bucketfuls of the animals: another way of controlling your snail population. But you need to feed them on clean lettuce and other decent grub for a week or so to clean out their systems before eating them; you never know what they might have just eaten. The old cookery books contain some fascinating recipes for cooking and serving them.

SIX LEGS: THE INSECTS

To the ordinary man-in-the-garden, an insect is any creepy-crawly with legs, but to the naturalist it is a creepy-crawly with just six legs in the adult state. Other obvious features include the division of the body into three main regions – head, thorax and abdomen – and the presence of a single pair of feelers or antennae on the head. Most insects also have two pairs of wings attached to the thorax in the adult state. No other group of invertebrates ever has wings, so all winged invertebrates are clearly insects; but the converse is not true – there are plenty of wingless insects, including all the young stages. About a million different kinds of insect have been discovered, with about 20,000 species in Britain and nearly 100,000 in Europe. They include such diverse creatures as dragonflies, earwigs, grasshoppers, greenfly, bees, ladybirds, butterflies and bluebottles. All belong to the even larger group known as the arthropods.

So what's an arthropod?

A creepy-crawly with legs! Our man-in-the-garden's definition of an insect is actually a pretty good definition of an arthropod. It is an invertebrate with a

INSECTS

have just three pairs of legs and a pair of feelers or antennae. The body is in three fairly distinct parts and there are usually wings. No other group of arthropod has wings, although there *are* many wingless insects.

ARTHROPODS

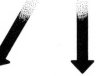

have segmented bodies clothed in a tough outer coat and bearing a number of jointed legs. Five main groups occur in the garden.

ARACHNIDS

have four pairs of legs. They include the spiders, seen here, with two body sections, and several smaller groups. There are never any antennae such as occur on other arthropods.

CRUSTACEANS

have relatively hard coats. The woodlice are the only garden-living representatives. They have seven pairs of legs.

MILLIPEDES

are herbivorous arthropods with cylindrical bodies and with two pairs of legs on most of the segments.

CENTIPEDES

are carnivorous arthropods with rather flat bodies and one pair of legs on each segment.

tough external skeleton covering a body which is usually clearly composed of rings or segments, and with a number of jointed legs, each enclosed in its own jointed skeleton, rather like a suit of *armour. Arthropod literally means 'jointed foot'. Apart from the insects, this immense group includes spiders, crabs, centipedes and millipedes.*

Insect life cycles

Most insects start life as eggs and they grow up with either a partial or a complete metamorphosis – a partial or complete change of form as they mature. Partial metamorphosis is shown by earwigs and grasshoppers, among many other insects: here the youngster is called a nymph and it resembles a small version of the adult except that it has no wings. The wings develop gradually as small 'buds' on the outside of the body, getting larger each time the insect changes its skin and reaching functional size at the final moult, when the insect becomes adult. Complete metamorphosis is shown by beetles, flies, butterflies and moths, and a few other groups; in this case the youngster looks nothing like the adult and is called a larva. It sometimes has six legs like the adult, but often has more than six and in many species has none at all. It often eats completely different food from the adult and may live a totally different life-style from that of the parent. There is no sign of wings, and when the larva changes its skin it simply becomes a bigger larva – until it reaches full size. Then it changes its skin again to reveal the pupa or chrysalis. This is a non-feeding and usually immobile stage of the life history, inside which great changes take place to convert the larval body into that of the adult. These remarkable changes can be completed in just a few days in some species, and the pupal skin then splits open for the winged adult to emerge.

New coats for old

The arthropod's outer skeleton, often hardened by impregnation with lime, gives the animal a good deal of protection, but it makes life a little tiresome in other respects. As a non-living coat, it does not grow with the animal, and so the arthropod's growth *has to take place in stages, punctuated by a number of skin changes or moults. When the young arthropod feels its skin getting tight, it stops feeding and becomes quiescent, often having sought a secluded spot in which to spend the next few vulnerable hours or days. Re-*

usable minerals are absorbed from the outer layer, which becomes progressively thinner and soon becomes detached from the underlying living skin. The animal then swallows air (or water if it is an aquatic beast) and its body swells up. The outer coat, now thin and papery, splits along the back and the animal hauls itself out. It has already grown a new coat, but this is still soft and much creased. Further swallowing of air or water irons out the wrinkles and the new coat gradually hardens, although it still retains a certain amount of elasticity. Elimination of the swallowed air or water makes room for another period of growth. Until the new coat has hardened the animal does not eat and it can't move or defend itself properly, so it's not surprising that moulting individuals generally hide themselves away.

The number of moults varies from species to species and may exceed fifty in some long-lived creatures, but the majority of insects undergo between three and ten moults. With a few exceptions, the insects do not grow or moult any more once they have reached maturity: small flies do not grow into larger flies.

Chirpy crickets

Crickets are related to grasshoppers and both groups are well known for the 'songs' that the males produce to attract and impress the ladies. Both groups have long back legs which they put to good use for leaping, but they are easily distinguished by their antennae: those of the grasshoppers are short and stout, while those of the crickets are long and slender – often much longer than the body. There are also differences in the method of song production: grasshoppers rub their hind legs on their wings to produce their chirps, while crickets rub their wing bases together. In addition, grasshoppers are active only in sunshine, whereas most crickets prefer to serenade us and their lady loves in the evenings and after dark.

The usual garden crickets are bush-crickets, which live up to their name by sneaking about in hedgerows and other dense vegetation. It is possible to track them down by listening to their calls – which are different for each species – but even then you'll be lucky to spot them, for they are exceedingly well camouflaged. Although the female has a fearsome-looking 'sword' at the rear, she is harmless at this end: the 'sword' is simply her egg-laying tool, with which she shoves her eggs into the soil or into crevices in plants. It's the front end that you have to watch: the larger species, such as the great green bush-cricket, will take lumps out of your fingers if you give them the

GARDEN CRICKETS

♂ = MALE   ♀ = FEMALE

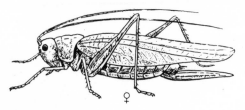

♀

GREET GREEN BUSH-CRICKET: deep green and up to 5 cm (2 in) long.
Song: long bursts of harsh hissing, rather like a high-pitched sewing machine.
Behaviour: largest and noisiest of the garden bush-crickets, it is widely distributed on the continent, but in Britain you are most likely to meet it south of the Thames, especially in coastal regions.

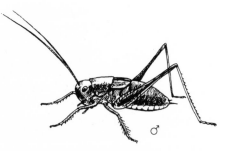

♂

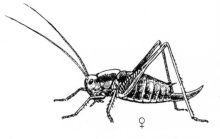

♀

DARK BUSH-CRICKET: light to dark brown and up to 2 cm (¾ inch) long.
Song: a soft *psst-psst-psst.*
Behaviour: a virtually wingless insect, apart from a couple of yellow flaps which the male retains for song production. It is often mistaken for a large spider as it crawls jerkily through the vegetation. Often enters houses in the autumn. It is common in many parts of southern Britain.

♀

♂

OAK BUSH-CRICKET: pale green and up to 1.7 cm (³/₅ inch) long.
Song: none.
Behaviour: lives in trees, unlike other British bush-crickets, and more often seen than heard. The male does not sing to attract a mate: he merely stamps his feet on a leaf to summon her. Both sexes commonly fly to lighted windows on autumn evenings. The male has unusually long claspers to embrace his chosen lady.

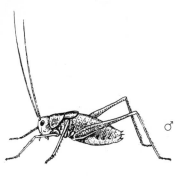 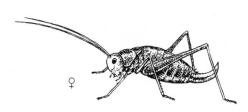

♂

♀

SPECKLED BUSH-CRICKET: speckled green and up to 1.7 cm (³/₅ inch) long.
Song: a very quiet chirp.
Behaviour: virtually wingless, apart from the tiny brown flaps on the top of the male's body. Probably the commonest garden bush-cricket, but so well camouflaged among the shrubs and herbaceous plants plants that it is rarely seen *or* heard. It is the only species likely to be found in Scottish gardens, and then only in the south-west.

chance. Left alone, however, they prefer to chew up other insects, garnished with the occasional leaf. All of our bush-crickets die in the autumn, leaving just their eggs to carry the species through the winter. Adults can be found from July until the autumn frosts. There is no chrysalis stage and the insects grow directly from nymphs into adults.

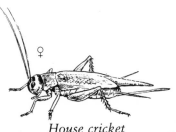

House cricket

The house cricket is one of the true crickets, differing from the bush crickets in several respects – notably the fine, needle-like egg-layer of the female. The house cricket used to be common in houses and was the familiar 'cricket on the hearth', but it is rarely found in such domestic situations today; even the hearth has gone from many houses. The insect's shrill, warbling chirp – music to some ears and an irritation to others – is now confined mainly to bakeries and large kitchens in Britain, although the cricket is well established on some rubbish dumps where its scavenging habits are well catered for and where decomposition provides the required warmth. During warm summers the insect may move into gardens, and during the 1976 drought its song could be heard coming from dried-out roadside drains in several parts of the country. The house cricket can be found all over Europe, but is most abundant in the warmer parts, in keeping with its Middle Eastern origin. Several other true crickets, with similarly shrill chirps, can be found in and around houses in southern Europe.

Outside jaws

With no bones, the insects and other arthropods obviously have no internal jaws to compare with our own. They deal with their food with the help of an array of external equipment collectively known as mouth-parts. These consist of a number of highly modified limbs surrounding the mouth and their form varies enormously – so much so that, between them, the insects can cope with every diet imaginable. There are biting mouth-parts that nibble, chew and crush solid foods before shoving them into the mouth, and there is a whole range of sucking mouth-parts designed for taking in liquids in conjunction with

The scorpion fly, seen here feeding from the body of a dead insect, carries its jaws at the end of a stout 'beak' under the head. The insect is harmless, despite the male's upturned, scorpion-like tail.

a pumping mechanism inside the mouth. In bugs and many flies some of the mouth-parts fit neatly together to form hypodermic needles, with which the insects pierce plants and other animals to get at the fluids. Other sucking mouth-parts are designed like sponges or drinking straws for mopping or sucking up free liquids. The house-flies and blow-flies have gone in for the sponge method and can actually use it on solid food by pouring digestive juices over the material and then mopping up the resulting solution. Bees and butterflies are masters of the 'drinking straw' technique.

Insect eyes

If you look at an insect with a strong lens, or better still with a microscope, you will see that the surface of each eye consists of numerous tiny hexagonal lenses. Eyes of this type are called compound eyes and they occur in several other types of arthropod as well as in the insects. Each lens forms its own image deep in the eye and the insect must therefore see a picture made up of numerous dots – one for each lens. The more lenses there are, the more detailed the picture will be. It will never be as good as the pictures produced by our own eyes, but the system is very good at picking up slight movements in the surroundings. A moving object stimulates a succession of lenses, making it easier for the insect to detect; and the larger the number of lenses, the better. A dragonfly, for example, which relies on sight to pick out its prey in mid-air, has some 30,000 lenses in each eye. A worker ant, on the other hand, which spends much of its time under the ground and which relies mainly on scent and touch to find its way about, may have only a few dozen lenses.

The maligned earwig

Every gardener knows the earwig, but few actually know anything about this abundant little insect. Most seem prepared to accept without question its terrible reputation as a piercer of ear drums and a destroyer of flowers and immediately put the boot in. As a youngster, it was some time before I felt brave enough to ignore parental warnings and have a good look at an earwig. I found not a savage fiend, but an engaging, if mischievous, little fellow with some truly fascinating habits. Sure, it will nibble a few prize flowers, and it probably will investigate your ears if you insist on sleeping on the ground, but it won't rip through your ear drum or hollow out your brain as people used to think. The worst it is likely to do is tickle you, and there is certainly no need to fear it. The earwig has a good case for misrepresentation and slander.

Europe's commonest earwig, and the only one commonly seen in British gardens, is *Forficula auricularia*, or the common earwig if you don't read Latin. It's dark brown, is between 10 and 15 mm ($^4/_{10}$ and $^6/_{10}$ inch) long and, like all earwigs, it carries a prominent pair of pincers at the rear. Generally 3–5 mm long, the pincers are slender and almost straight in the female but stouter and strongly curved in the male, who uses them on occasion to wrestle with rival males. They are primarily defensive weapons, however, and if you pick up an earwig by the front end the pincers will curve round to nip you. They can exert quite a force, although they can't hurt you: only an inquisitive shrew or hedgehog need fear for its nose.

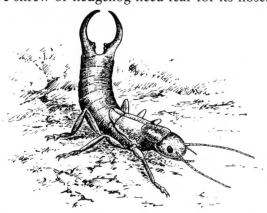

A male earwig threatens to use his powerful pincers.

If you've never seen an earwig fly you're in good company: few people ever have. It's a reluctant aeronaut, but the insect *can* fly – when it manages to get its wings out. The front wings are small leathery flaps, which you can see just behind the head, and the hind wings, which actually get the thing airborne, are elaborately folded beneath them. There may be as many as forty thicknesses of the wing, folded fan-like under the front wings, so packing and unpacking them is quite a perfomance and the insect may need several attempts before the wings are satisfactorily stowed. The pincers are often used in this operation. The hind wings are extraordinarily thin and seem too flimsy to support even an earwig, but the insect somehow manages to stay aloft. The small earwig (*Labia minor*) flies more readily than its larger

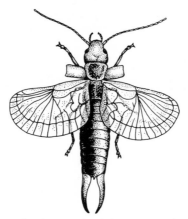

A female earwig displaying the delicate, ear-shaped hind wings.

cousin but, although widely distributed, it is rarely noticed. Look for it in and around the compost heap. It is pale brown and only 4–8 mm long.

Earwigs eat more or less anything they can lay their jaws on – plant or animal, living or dead. They are real scavengers and are not averse to a bit of cannibalism when other food is scarce. They nibble growing plants, especially flowers and fruits, but make up for this minor damage by eating a variety of small caterpillars and other garden pests, including large numbers of aphids. The pincers are sometimes used to subdue more lively victims, such as flies, although it is unlikely that many flies are caught in the wild. I have seen the pincers used for prey capture only when keeping earwigs in small boxes, from which the flies had no escape. The earwigs don't exert themselves any more than they have to, and they concentrate on static or slow-moving food sources. I have seen several sit down together to dine on a batch of moth eggs, and some years ago a Dr Eltringham described how an earwig sat by a yellow underwing moth and ate the moth's eggs as they were being laid. Dead insects are also eagerly consumed, and many an insect collection has suffered from earwig damage when boxes have not been properly closed.

Earwigs are nocturnal creatures and spend the daytime snugly tucked up in an assortment of nooks and crannies. Just as we like to snuggle down between the sheets, the earwig likes to wriggle into narrow crevices where it can feel both back and belly in contact with something. Loose bark is a favourite resting site, and if you leave an old cloth draped over a branch or a log for a few weeks you will probably find numerous earwigs taking up residence. It's also worth having a look at the seed capsules of granny-bonnets or columbines in the autumn, for these also shelter lots of earwigs. In my own garden the capsules are commonly occupied by *Apterygida media*, a flightless species with no hind wings. The male has long, slender pincers which are not flattened like those of the common earwig. The tubular florets of dahlias and chrysanthemums also make comfortable bedrooms for earwigs, much to the consternation of gardeners preparing their blooms for the flower show. Damage to the flowers is usually slight, and you can reduce it even further by providing alternative sleeping accommodation for the insects. The traditional method is to stuff flower pots with straw and fix them upside-down among the flowers. The earwigs readily occupy the pots, especially if you daub the straw with honey, and you can release them well away from your flowers in the morning.

Whereas most insects never have any contact with their offspring, lady earwigs are extremely attentive mothers, lavishing care on their eggs and babies for several months. Mating generally takes place in the autumn, and the earwigs seek snug winter quarters at the first hint of frost. Most of them head for the soil, where they hollow out comfortable bed-chambers under logs and stones. Being quite sociable creatures, considerable numbers often gather together to bed down in the best sites – package tourism is nothing new.

The female lays her eggs in the winter retreat and guards them lovingly, lying over them and periodically licking them all to keep them free from

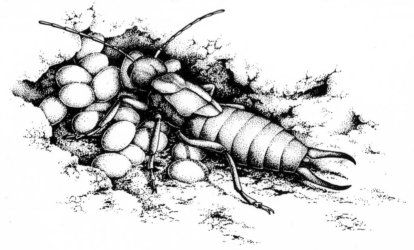

A female earwig tending her eggs.

mould and bacteria. The eggs die if they are removed from the mother for any length of time, but if you give them back to her after a short while she gathers them up and fusses over them like a human mother re-united with lost children. The eggs hatch in the spring, but the mother does not relax her vigil. She continues to clean her babies just as she did her eggs, and she even feeds them with material regurgitated from her own stomach. The nymphs leave their birthplace after the second moult (in late spring/early summer) and start to feed themselves, but they keep close to mother and scurry for the shelter of her body if they are disturbed. All twenty or thirty of them try to get round her, like a litter of piglets scrapping for places at the milk-bar. They are paler than the adults and have much more slender pincers. The wings are visible only as small pads on the back and do not reach full size until the fourth and final moult, which usually occurs in mid-summer. The family then begins to break up and the mother dies – after a life of about eighteen months. Freshly moulted earwigs are creamy white and are mistakenly thought to be albinos when they are discovered under logs and stones.

Why earwig?

No-one really knows why they are called earwigs, but several ideas have been put forward to explain the name. One is that it is a corruption of

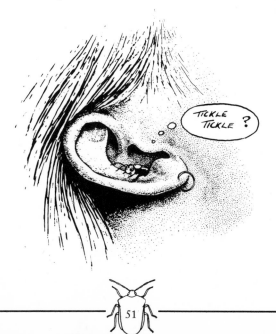

'ear-wing' and refers to the ear-like shape of the unfolded hind wing. On the face of it, this seems a logical explanation, but with so few people ever seeing the insect's hind wings – or even realizing that they exist – I can't see the name developing in this way. In addition, this idea does not explain the French *perce-oreille* (ear-piercer) or the German *ohrwurm* (ear-worm). Another suggestion is that the name arose from the likeness of the male's pincers to the instrument once used for piercing ladies' ear-lobes, but the most likely explanation is that the name is derived from the insects' interest in the human ear as a resting place. We might not get many earwigs in our ears today, but in the past, when straw mattresses and thatched roofs were common, such occurrences were undoubtedly much more frequent.

A load of suckers

The word bug is commonly used for any kind of insect, and insect collectors have long been dubbed bug-hunters, but the name really belongs just to

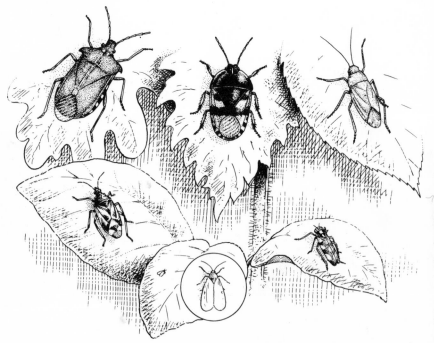

A selection of garden bugs: (clockwise from top left) *forest bug; pied shield bug; common green capsid; common flower bug; white fly; potato leafhopper.*

members of the large order known as the Hemiptera. These true bugs include a wide range of winged and wingless insects, embracing shield bugs, bed bugs, water boatmen, froghoppers, aphids and many more. Their habits are as different as their looks, but the one thing they all have in common is a needle-like beak with which they pierce plants or other animals and suck out the juices. Most are plant-feeders, but some attack other insects and a few take blood from larger creatures, including us. Hemiptera literally means 'half-wing' and refers to the nature of the front wing in many of the species: the basal part of the wing is tough and horny, while the outer part is membranous. Just to confuse you further, however, many bugs have entirely horny or entirely membranous front wings.

The bugs all grow up without a pupal stage, the nymphs looking very much like small adults except that the wings are present as no more than small flaps on the back. Nymphs and young generally feed on the same kinds of food and are commonly present together.

Bug or beetle?

The tough front wings of many bugs, sheathing the body and completely covering the hind wings, give the insects a superficial similarity to beetles, but you have only to look under the head to distinguish the two groups. The slender beak, often folded back between the front legs, immediately tells you that you are looking at a bug. A membranous wing-tip also identifies the insect as a bug: although not all bugs have this feature, you never find it among the beetles.

A bug has a slender, piercing beak.

A beetle has biting jaws.

A bug's front wings commonly overlap in the middle, and the membranous tip is commonly clearly visible.

A beetle's tough front wings meet in the middle, forming a protective sheath.

The most abundant and familiar of the garden bugs are the aphids – the troublesome greenfly and blackfly and their relatives. There are both winged and wingless individuals in each species, but when wings are present they are completely membranous. Although the individuals are small, they exist in immense numbers and cause severe damage to plants by removing large quantities of sap and by spreading virus diseases, such as potato leaf roll. Few plant species are without at least one kind of aphid, and in a rich natural community it has been estimated that there may be more than 5,000,000,000 aphids per hectare (2,000,000,000 per acre).

Aphids feed entirely by puncturing the plants and sucking out the sap. The latter is rich in sugars but has a very low protein content, and in order to get sufficient protein the insects have to take in far more sugar than they can use. The excess is simply pumped out at the other end as honeydew – the sticky deposit that covers aphid-infested plants and, as any car driver can tell you, anything that happens to be underneath them. Never park your car

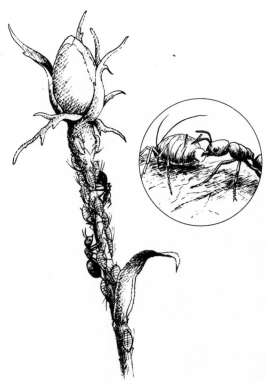

Black ants 'milking' aphids for honeydew.

under sycamore or lime trees in the summer, for these trees have particularly high aphid populations and honeydew literally rains from them at times. In some dry regions of the world the water evaporates rapidly from the honeydew, leaving clumps of crystallized sugar which people collect and eat as manna. Ants are very partial to honeydew. They collect large amounts from the leaves, and many species also 'milk' the aphids to get fresh drinks on demand. Many other insects, including bees and wasps and some butterflies, also lap honeydew from the leaves. Any deposits that are not eaten are rapidly infected by a black fungus, which turns all the leaves black in the summer. Much of the honeydew falls to the ground, however, and here it can repay some of the damage which the aphids have done to the plants. Recent research has shown that the sugars washed into the soil may stimulate bacterial activity, leading to the production of extra nitrates – which promote better growth when absorbed by the plant roots.

Many aphid species spend their entire lives on one kind of plant, or on a group of closely related plants, but some, including most of the serious pests, alternate between two entirely different host plants. For much of the year they do without sex. In fact, there are only females around for much of the time and they go in for virgin birth, producing babies rather than eggs.

Generation after generation of females are produced during the summer, with some individuals giving birth to more than ten youngsters in a single day. The youngsters undergo four moults in quick succession and are ready to give birth themselves in less than a couple of weeks. Because all the aphids are female and all can give birth, the numbers build up extremely quickly during spring and summer. If a female gave birth to 50 babies – not an unreasonable average for most species – and all her descendants survived to reproduce, there would be more than 6,000,000 aphids from this one individual within two months. It's a good job there are plenty of natural enemies around, in the form of ladybirds, lacewings and insectivorous birds; without them we would be buried by aphids and all the plants would be sucked dry.

The life cycle of the black bean aphid (*Aphis fabae*), better known in the garden simply as blackfly, will give a good idea of the complexities of aphid life. In common with most other aphids, it spends the winter in the egg stage – although you can also find adults on various plants in areas with mild winters. The eggs are laid on the bark of spindle and guelder rose bushes and also on the cultivated mock orange. They hatch in the spring and the young nymphs quickly plug in to the opening buds. All grow into wingless females, and before long they produce their own families – more wingless blackfly clustering densely on the young leaves and shoots. Reproduction speeds up as spring temperatures rise, and winged individuals begin to put in an appearance. Crowding seems to be the main factor involved in producing winged individuals: the more the young nymphs bump into each other, the more likely they are to grow up into winged adults. Changes in the nature of the plant sap may also play a part, but, whatever the cause, more and more winged aphids develop as time goes by and they gradually fly off to other plants; not to more bushes, but to the succulent tips of our beans and beet.

Virgin birth continues on the herbaceous plants, leading to dense colonies of blackfly and considerable damage to leaves and shoots. The new insects are all wingless at first but, as the crowds build up, winged individuals appear again and fly off to continue the population explosion on other plants. Many wild plants, such as docks and poppies, are affected just as much as our garden plants. The build-up goes on until early autumn, when a change comes over the aphids. Shorter days, lower temperatures and a deterioration in the quality of the plant sap combine to persuade many of the winged adults to fly back to the spindle and other host bushes, where they give birth to special egg-laying females. Only now does sex come into the aphids' lives. The dwindling colonies left on the summer host plants produce winged males, which fly to the bushes and seek out the wingless, egg-laying females. During their short lives, measured in hours rather than days, the males mate with several females, and the latter then each lay about half a dozen eggs. Many eggs are eaten by blue tits and other birds during the winter, but sufficient survive to ensure that we are invaded by blackfly again in the following summer.

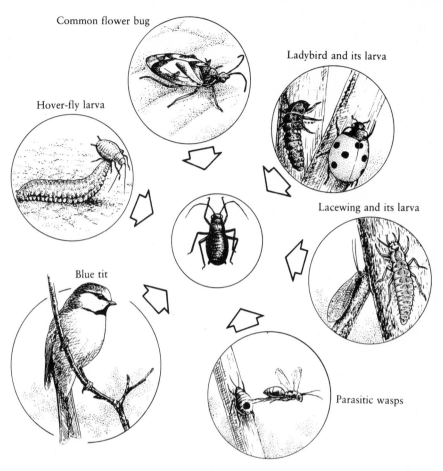

Common flower bug

Ladybird and its larva

Hover-fly larva

Lacewing and its larva

Blue tit

Parasitic wasps

Who'd be an aphid with all these enemies?

Other all-too-familiar garden aphids with similar two-host life cycles include the rose aphid or greenfly (*Macrosiphum rosae*) and the peach-potato aphid (*Myzus persicae*). The former is a plump green or pink aphid with long black legs and cornicles (see p. 59). It infests rose buds and shoots in the spring and then transfers its attention to scabious and teasel plants for the summer. The peach-potato aphid is pale green or yellow with black markings and it causes peach leaves to curl in the spring – although it is not the only culprit in this respect. As spring turns into summer the aphid moves to potatoes, cabbages and many other herbaceous plants. It rarely forms dense colonies, but the total population is very high. In mild winters the species can carry on reproducing by parthenogenesis (virgin birth), but in the colder parts of its range it must return to the peach tree to produce its eggs. In tropical regions the species seem to have abandoned sexual reproduction and egg-laying altogether.

Aphid swarms

We sometimes experience immense swarms of aphids in the summer, with the insects literally getting into everything. Several species may be involved, and several factors may contribute to the build-up of numbers, but the most recent widespread 'plague' in Britain was in 1979, when countless millions of rose-grain aphids (Metopolophium dirhodum) came off the cereal crops in July. These were the aphids that clogged up my garden spider webs (see p. 126). Numbers were able to build up to such immense populations on this occasion largely because the previous winter was very severe and killed off a high proportion of ladybirds and other aphid enemies.

The cabbage aphid (*Brevicoryne brassicae*) is troublesome in many gardens, especially in early summer when the brassicas have just been planted out. Winged individuals sniff out the young plants right away and quickly settle down to produce dense colonies of wingless grey aphids, all clothed with a waxy powder. Whole plants may be smothered, and many give up and die. Infested leaves should be removed and burnt as soon as you see the colonies developing. Pale, crinkly patches are often the first sign that the aphids are busy. If the infestation is allowed to continue, winged individuals will soon be produced and will fly off to infest other plants. All the cabbage tribe are at risk, and the aphid can also flourish on weeds such as shepherd's purse. There is no migration to a woody host plant in the autumn and the aphids spend their entire life cycle on brassicas and related plants. The winter is passed in the egg stage in cold climates, but in warmer areas the aphids can remain active throughout the year. Pull up and destroy old brassica stems as soon as you have finished with them in the winter, thereby destroying many eggs and aphids which would otherwise flourish and attack the next season's crops.

Apple growers need no introduction to the woolly aphid (*Eriosoma lanigerum*), sometimes known as American blight because of its transatlantic origin. It is responsible for the fluffy white tufts that burst from apple branches in the spring and early summer – usually from cuts or other wounded surfaces. Remove the waxy fluff, and you will reveal the massed purplish brown bodies of the aphids, all busily sucking sap. Squashing them is the best control method for small infestations, for the waxy threads produced by the insects protect them from all but the heaviest applications of insecticide. The European population consists entirely of females, so no sexual reproduction takes place and no eggs are laid. Young aphids pass the winter in bark crevices, from where many are plucked by foraging blue tits, and the colonies build up again in the spring. Relatively few winged individuals are produced and the infestations tend to be localized on single trees or groups of neighbouring trees.

Chemical warnings

Look at the rear end of most aphids and you will see a pair of slender horns, known as cornicles or siphunculi. Once thought to release honeydew, they are now known to be concerned with protecting the aphids from insect enemies, especially from parasites and from those predators that are about the same size as the aphids. When an aphid is attacked by one of these enemies it exudes a waxy fluid from its cornicles and endeavours to plaster it on the attacker's face. As the wax solidifies rapidly on exposure to the air, it acts as an effective deterrent – just like a custard pie in the face according to one author! But the fluid does more than simply ward off an attacker. Its odour

actually warns neighbouring aphids that danger is about. Experiments have shown that release of the fluid makes *nearby aphids crawl away or drop to the ground, thereby getting themselves out of the firing line.*

Oh spit!

The little blobs of white froth that mysteriously appear on various plants in the spring are commonly known as cuckoo-spit, although they have nothing to do with cuckoos. They are produced by the nymphs of some little brown bugs called froghoppers or spittle bugs. The adult bug looks vaguely like a tiny frog, and leaps just as well for its size. The female lays her eggs in the plant stems and the nymphs emerge the following spring. Having found a juicy stem, each nymph settles down to feed and soon starts to pump fluid out at the rear. This fluid contains

a soapy secretion from the excretory system, and by pumping air into it from a small cavity under the abdomen the insect causes it to froth up. The froth protects the nymph from desiccation and also from various potential enemies, although some solitary wasps have learned that there is a meal under all the bubbles.

So why cuckoo-spit? The name is simply an old one, given before the true nature of the froth was known. Because it appears at about the time of year that the cuckoo arrives, it is quite logical for the two to be linked.

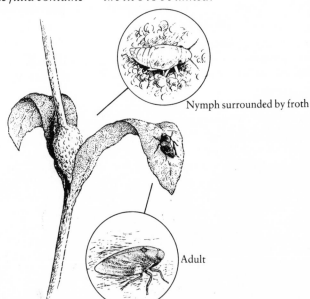

Nymph surrounded by froth

Adult

The cuckoo-spit insect or common froghopper.

Butterfly gardening

Apart from the destructive cabbage whites, butterflies are among the most welcome of garden visitors. Flitting from flower to flower, they are the dancers that bring your colourful stage to life. About a dozen species are regular visitors to our gardens, in the town as well as in the country. Many more may fly through, or even stop off for a drink, if your garden is close to woodland or other uncultivated habitats. The common garden species are shown in the accompanying chart.

Butterflies are all nectar-feeders and will very often let you get close enough to watch their long tongues in action, snaking out from under the head and probing deep into the flowers to suck up the nectar. Over-ripe apples and other fruits attract some butterflies, especially the handsome red admiral – which gets so drunk on the fermented juices that you can often pick it up in your fingers. It's always worth leaving a few fallen fruits on the ground to attract butterflies, but for a real butterfly ball you need a succession of nectar-rich flowers from early spring until the autumn frosts. The butterfly's tongue is long enough to reach the nectar in most flowers, as long as it is not hidden behind trap-doors or other cunning devices, and most cultivated species fit the bill. But avoid the 'giant, new, improved' varieties. Bred to provide maximum colour, these monsters often have no nectar because the nectaries have been lost; even if they do have nectar it is often way out of reach of the butterflies' tongues. The old-fashioned, cottage garden flowers are usually the best butterfly attractants, and the following types, arranged in order of flowering from spring to autumn, are among my own favourites:

Aubretia, which carpets walls and rockeries with pink or lilac flowers in the spring, is the best of the early flowers, providing a good feast of nectar for the small tortoiseshell and other species that hibernate as adults and wake up hungry in the spring sunshine. Its long flowering period also means that it is still around to nourish the orange tip and other butterflies that emerge later in the spring. Wallflowers and polyanthus are also worth planting as butterfly attractants for early spring. Honesty and sweet rocket come high on my list for May, mainly because of their attraction for the orange-tip. Adult butterflies feed at the flowers, and the females also lay their eggs amongst them, leaving the beautifully camouflaged caterpillars to feed on the developing seed capsules. The green-veined white, not a pest like its two cousins, also enjoys the sweet rocket.

The long flowering season of red valerian makes it an ideal plant for the

THE COMMON GARDEN BUTTERFLIES AND THEIR CATERPILLARS

The butterflies illustrated are all males: females are similar unless otherwise stated. All are shown about half size.

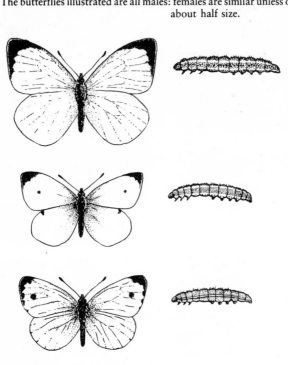

LARGE WHITE Female has black spots on front wing. Flies April–September. Caterpillar on cabbages and nasturtiums. Passes winter as a chrysalis.

SMALL WHITE Female has two black spots on front wing. Flies March–October. Caterpillar on cabbages and nasturtiums. Passes winter as a chrysalis.

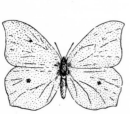

GREEN-VEINED WHITE Female has two black spots on front wing. Flies April–September. Caterpillar on cruciferous weeds such as charlock. Passes winter as a chrysalis.

ORANGE-TIP Male has bright orange wing-tips. Flies April–June. Caterpillar on cuckoo flower, garlic mustard, and other crucifers – including honesty. Passes winter as a chrysalis.

BRIMSTONE Male is bright yellow; female is pale greenish white. Flies March–September. Caterpillar on buckthorn and alder buckthorn. Passes winter as hibernating adult.

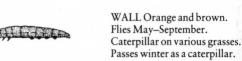

WALL Orange and brown. Flies May–September. Caterpillar on various grasses. Passes winter as a caterpillar.

HOLLY BLUE Male is violet-blue; female is paler blue with broad black margins. Flies April–September. Caterpillar on holly (spring) and ivy (autumn). Passes winter as a chrysalis.

SMALL COPPER Bright orange with dark brown or black markings. Flies April–October. Caterpillar on dock and sorrel. Passes winter as a caterpillar.

SMALL TORTOISESHELL Orange and black with dotted blue borders. Flies March–October. Caterpillar on stinging nettle. Passes winter as hibernating adult.

PEACOCK Mostly red and black, with blue in 'eyes'. Flies March–September. Caterpillar on stinging nettle. Passes winter as hibernating adult.

RED ADMIRAL Velvety black with broad red stripes and white spots. Flies May–October. Caterpillar on stinging nettle. A summer visitor to British Isles.

PAINTED LADY Orange with black and white markings. Flies May–October. Caterpillar on thistles and occasionally nettles. A summer visitor to British Isles.

COMMA Orange-brown with darker markings. Flies March–October. Caterpillar on hop, stinging nettle and elm. Passes winter as hibernating adult.

butterfly garden, although it can be rather invasive. Most butterflies will drink its nectar, and so will many moths – including the day-flying hummingbird hawk moth, which is normally seen as a brownish blur in front of the flowers. Lavender will attract any butterfly that's about, while the drawing power of the buddleia is almost legendary. Having arrived from China less than a century ago, it can hardly be called a cottage garden plant, but it fits nicely into even a very small garden and will repay you handsomely with its flowers as well as with the butterflies it brings in. I have recorded more than thirty species feeding on the flowers, with a recent highlight being the presence of nine species on a single branch at the same time. Try to plant at least two varieties, with slightly different flowering periods.

Hebe, a shrubby relative of the speedwell, is not quite in the buddleia league, but still worth planting for its long-lasting sprays of purple or white flowers. Shaped like bottle brushes, they are sweetly scented and bring in plenty of butterflies and other insects. There are several different species flowering throughout the summer.

Best of all the autumn-flowering plants is undoubtedly the ice plant (*Sedum spectabile*), whose broad pink flower heads serve dinner to hordes of small tortoiseshells stocking up for the winter. Commas, red admirals and painted ladies may also join the feast. Michaelmas daisies take over when the ice plant fades, and continue to nourish the butterflies on sunny days until the end of October, when the last tortoiseshells finally decide it's time to sleep.

Butterflies are generally quite sociable when feeding, as you can see from the numbers on a single buddleia spray or ice plant head: as long as each has room to spread its wings, they are usually content to dine together. There are some less gregarious species, however, in which the individuals like to play 'king of the castle'. Each butterfly adopts a flower or a cluster of flowers as its territory and chases off any other butterfly that attempts to invade its privacy. The small copper frequently behaves like this on Michaelmas daisies, but it doesn't necessarily patrol the same territory each day: individuals squabble over their territories each morning to establish ownership for the day, and they obviously move their territories around as new flowers open.

You can see from the chart on pp. 62–3 that the only regular breeders in a typical garden are likely to be the large and small whites – the cabbage whites whose caterpillars do so much damage to our brassicas. Although

closely related, the two species have rather different habits in the larval stage. The large white lays its bright yellow eggs in large clusters under the leaves, and the black and yellow larvae remain together for most of their lives, feeding conspicuously on the leaves. They have a foul taste and odour – which you can smell several paces away from a heavy infestation – and their bold colours warn birds of their unpalatability. Young birds will try them, but quickly learn that black and yellow caterpillars are nasty and are to be left alone. This is just one of many examples of warning coloration to be seen in the garden. Wasps and ladybirds protect themselves in the same way. The small white goes in for camouflage rather than advertisement. lays its eggs singly, often on the upper side of a leaf, but they are pale green and not easily spotted. The caterpillars are also pale green and they live singly, usually resting along the leaf veins which they resemble very closely. The camouflage might not fool all the insect's enemies, but many caterpillar escapes the cook's eye and ends up on the dinner table. Luckily for our cabbages, and for us, the cabbage white caterpillars have many enemies which can sniff them out and which are undeterred by the awful flavour of the large white larvae. In the vanguard of the attack are some tiny parasites related to the ichneumon flies (see p. 112), which lay their eggs inside the caterpillars. The resulting grubs gradually destroy the caterpillar from the inside, with affected individuals becoming very lethargic. When they die you can see the parasites' yellow cocoons clustering around the empty skins.

If you have holly or ivy in your garden you might persuade the holly blue to breed, and long grass along the hedge or in the orchard might encourage the wall brown, although neither species ventures very far into Scotland. The orange-tip will also breed on honesty and sweet rocket, but if you want to do your conservation bit for the peacocks and tortoiseshells you must provide a bed of stinging nettles – not the most attractive of garden feature unless you happen to be a caterpillar. The spiky larvae of the peacock and small tortoiseshell feed gregariously for much of their lives, spinning untidy silken tents over the nettles. Red admirals and commas may also be grateful for your nettle patch, and painted ladies may also breed there, although they prefer thistles. To be of any real use, however, your nettle patch must be in the sun for at least part of the day. The female butterflies lay their eggs only in the sunshine, and a permanently shaded nettle bed will never attract them.

Winter butterflies

Another look at the chart on pp. 62–3 will reveal that four of our garden butterflies pass the winter in the adult state. These are the first to appear in the spring, woken from their slumbers on sunny days as early as February. The natural hibernation sites of the peacock and small tortoiseshell include caves and hollow trees, where they are well concealed by their sombre undersides, but the insects are now happy to move into garden sheds and other out-buildings and also into attics and other little-used rooms. They often wake up when the central heating is turned up in the middle of winter, and if you find them flying around the house at this time the best thing is to put them in the shed or the garage where they can go back to sleep again. The brimstone prefers to take its winter sleep in evergreen shrubs, especially amongst holly or ivy leaves. Its strongly veined, leaf-like underside camouflages it remarkably well. The comma beds down in any dense shrub or undergrowth, where its jagged outline and dark underside enable it to masquerade as a dead leaf. These hibernating butterflies live for nine months or so.

Beautiful migrants

Many butterflies migrate, and several species occur in Britain and other parts of northern Europe only as summer visitors from the south. The red admiral is a well known example. Resident in southern Europe, it spreads

northwards in the spring, reaching far into Scandinavia and producing a summer generation wherever it finds stinging nettles. There is some southward movement of these summer butterflies in the autumn, but most succumb to the first frosts. A few lucky ones may find sufficiently warm sleeping quarters for the winter, but successful hibernation in northern areas is extremely rare, if it occurs at all. Evolution may produce a cold-hardy race one day, and then this beautiful butterfly will perhaps become a permanent resident. The painted lady has a similar life cycle although it is even less hardy than the red admiral. It comes up from North Africa each spring and a fair number make the return flight in the autumn although the majority of European-born butterflies still die without issue.

Living ornaments

It's fashionable in some circles to have butterflies and some of the larger and showier moths flying around the house. They're undeniably attractive and great conversation pieces but, unless you can perpetuate your stock by breeding – and this means providing plenty of space, nectar-rich flowers and larval foodplants – I am not in favour of this type of 'pet'. The insects should certainly never be taken from the wild for such a purpose. Most 'household' butterflies are, of course, exotic species bought from dealers, but this doesn't mean that there is no drain on the wild stocks. Reputable dealers breed their own supplies and have due regard for conservation, but there is still a considerable trade in butterflies and many are becoming rare in their original home – although in some areas people are realizing the value of butterflies as a 'crop' and breed them on 'butterfly ranches' for export. There is also the problem of escapes. Tropical species

are unlikely to survive in our climate but hardier insects could establish themselves and interfere with our native wildlife. It is now an offence under the Wildlife and Countryside Act to introduce alien species into the British countryside.

Introducing native butterflies to your garden might seem like a good idea, and seed firms used to offer the pupae of various species for sale along with their seeds and other garden materials. But again there are problems. Being nomadic creatures, the butterflies are unlikely to stay in your garden for long and, unless the right food plants are available in the area, the insects will quickly die out. In short, you're wasting your money. If local conditions are right, the butterflies will exist in your area anyway, and if you make your garden sufficiently attractive – by planting lots of nectar-rich flowers – they will come along of their own accord.

Moths in the garden

Moths are a good deal less obvious than butterflies because the majority fly about at night, but you have only to wander round your flower garden with a torch at night to realize just how many moths live in or visit the garden. Many can be found sitting on or hovering in front of the flowers and drinking nectar, although quite a few moths have no functional tongue and take no food at all in the adult state. Females flitting from leaf to leaf are likely to be looking for egg-laying sites, for a great many kinds of moth breed in the garden – although relatively few have caterpillars that do much damage to our flowers and crops. The cabbage moth is one of the worst pests. Its plump, dirty green or brownish larvae tunnel deep into cabbages in summer and autumn and, although they might not actually eat much of a cabbage, their smell and their accumulated droppings render large amounts unfit for the table. Fully-grown caterpillars pupate in the soil, and the bullet-shaped chestnut brown pupae are commonly dug up in the vegetable plot. But not all such pupae belong to the cabbage moth: many species pupate in the soil and their pupae are very difficult to distinguish.

Most moths sleep during the daytime, either hiding amongst the vegetation or resting openly on tree trunks and walls. Those sleeping in the open rely on camouflage to escape the attentions of birds and other enemies, and experiments have shown that the moths really do pick out surfaces that afford the best protection. They also align their patterns with the bark crevices for even greater concealment and security, although this isn't quite as clever as it seems. Most bark crevices run more or less vertically, and the moths have merely evolved resting positions in which their own patterns also run vertically. But camouflage goes deeper than simply blending in with the background. Many moths have evolved shapes and attitudes which give them more than passing resemblances to broken twigs or slivers of bark, while others, especially those that rest amongst the herbage, are easily taken for dead leaves. Even such a large moth as the poplar hawk, up to 90 mm (3½ inches) across the wings, can be overlooked in this way.

Some of our garden moths seem to sleep much more soundly than others during the day, and you can prod them quite a bit before they do more than shrug their shoulders. They may walk a few steps and then settle down again, and only prolonged nudging will cause them to take flight. On the other hand there are those that take flight at the slightest disturbance. The large yellow underwing is a good example, commonly put up from the herbaceous borders in the summer. But it is extremely difficult to follow in flight, taking an erratic, zig-zag course and flashing its bright yellow hind wings as it goes. Then it drops to the ground quite suddenly and conceals the yellow with its drab brown front wings, leaving the gardener scratching his head in puzzlement. Birds are equally deceived into searching for a bright yellow insect, and the moth escapes – unfortunately for the gardener for its plump green or brown caterpillar, up to 5 cm (2 inches) long, can do a lot of damage to both flowers and vegetables. It is one of a group known as cut-worms, living in the upper layers of the soil and emerging at night to nibble a wide variety of plant stems, often cutting right through them at ground level and allowing slugs to take the blame. You can find the caterpillars at work on mild nights right through the winter. They pupate in the soil in the spring.

The aptly-named eyed hawkmoth, which is not uncommon on apple trees in the garden, literally frightens off any small bird that disturbs it. Raising its sombre front wings, it exposes two large and very realistic eye-spots on its hind wings, and at the same time it heaves its body up and down. It must be quite a shock to a bird to find itself suddenly face to face with a good impression of an owl or a pussy cat, and the bird beats a hasty retreat.

The lives of butterflies and moths

Butterflies and moths all belong to the large group of insects called Lepidoptera. The name means 'scale-wings', for the insects' wings are clothed with minute scales that provide their colour and pattern. As far as the British

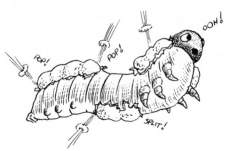

Caterpillars have to change their skins on several occasions during their lives (see p. 42).

and European species are concerned, the easiest way to separate the butterflies from the moths is to look at the antennae. The butterfly antenna always ends in a small knob. It is never hair-like or feathery like that of many moths. Some moths have clubbed antennae, but they usually thicken gradually towards the tip, not abruptly as in the butterflies.

The butterflies and moths all have similar life cycles, beginning with eggs and passing through caterpillar and chrysalis stages before becoming adult. Some species have two or even three generations in a year, but most have just one. A few moths take two or more years to grow up. Species living in southern Britain may have two generations in a year, while the same species may have only one generation in the cooler climate of the north.

Most butterfly chrysalids either hang by the tail end or are held vertically on a support by a silken girdle. Moth chrysalids (right) lie in a silken cocoon or in an underground chamber.

Day-flying moths

It is commonly said that butterflies are brightly coloured and fly by day, while moths are drab and fly by night. Butterflies obey this 'rule' quite well, but nobody seems to have told the moths about it. Many species, including the brilliantly marked tiger moths, are as bright as any butterfly, and a fair number fly by day. The hummingbird hawkmoth is a well known daytime visitor to the flower garden, although all that you normally see is a brown blur hovering in front of the blooms – just like a hummingbird. If you can get close enough you will see the long tongue probing the flowers for nectar, but the moth generally zooms away before you can get a good look. A summer visitor from southern Europe, it is abundant in Britain and other northern regions in some years and scarce in others. It tucks itself up in sheds or in crevices in walls and tree trunks for the night, and the occasional specimen may survive the northern winter in such places. The silver-Y is a much more abundant summer visitor – and a tireless one, for it seems to be on the wing at all hours of day and night. During the daytime, when it mingles with the butterflies on the buddleia and other flowers, it is often mistaken for the hummingbird hawkmoth, for it rarely sits still and, although it may cling to the petals with its front legs, its wings continue to beat rapidly. But the blur is greyer than that of the hummingbird hawkmoth and the insect doesn't shoot off quite so readily. If it does sit still you can see the mottled grey wings and the silvery Y-shaped mark that gives the moth its name. The green caterpillar feeds on a wide range of garden plants and, like its close relatives, has only three pairs of fleshy legs at the rear instead of five.

The hummingbird hawkmoth feeding at a flower.

Moths in the winter

Many people are surprised to see moths sitting on window panes on cold winter nights, even when it is foggy or when the temperature is hovering at or below freezing. With no flowers around to provide nectar, conditions are far from ideal for moths, and yet several species have selected this spartan life style. The commonest visitor to the window pane is the winter moth, a small greyish brown insect that will sit there for hours as long as the light stays on (see p. 78). All are males, for the female is a wingless, spidery creature which must be sought on the trunks of apples and other garden trees. Those males that are not distracted by our lights mate with the females on the trees and the mated females then climb up to lay their eggs on the twigs. The slender green caterpillars strip the young leaves in the spring and then tunnel into the ground to pupate. Adults emerge mainly between

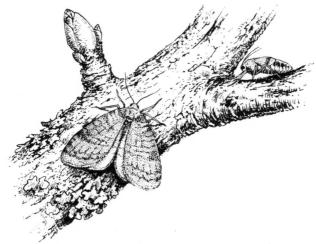

The male winter moth (left) *approaches the wingless female.*

November and February. In November and December the males are often joined on the window panes by the mottled umber, a larger and browner moth with a similar life history. Although not all winter-flying moths have wingless females, there are distinct advantages to this arrangement. Flight requires a good deal of energy, and with no nectar on hand to replenish it all the energy must come from food already stored in the body. By doing away with flight, the wingless females can concentrate all their energy on egg production, which is clearly an advantage for the species.

The garden ghost

Stroll around your garden at dusk in June or July and you might well meet a ghost. But don't worry: it's only a moth. The male ghost swift moth is pure white on the upper side and dark brown below, and you see just flashes of white as it flies. Its habit of dancing slowly up and down at about head height gives it an even more ghostly appearance. This unusual flight attracts the yellowish females, which scatter their eggs over the garden after mating. The

caterpillars feed on roots of all kinds and may do considerable damage to the lawn and the herbaceous garden. The white plume moth also has a ghostly flight, although it is much smaller than the ghost swift. It is most often seen on window panes on summer evenings, and then you can easily see why it is called a plume moth: the pure white wings are each broken up into delicate 'feathers'. The caterpillar feeds on bindweed.

Caterpillars: camouflage and advertisement

Moth caterpillars can be found on most garden plants, although they are not usually very conspicuous. Like the adults, many of them rely on camouflage to escape detection. Many a caterpillar has been brought into the house unseen on cut flowers, revealing its presence only when its droppings accumulate under the vase – and even then the culprit might take some tracking down by the inexpert eye. You wouldn't think that a privet hawkmoth caterpillar, up to 8 cm (just over 3 inches) long, could hide very

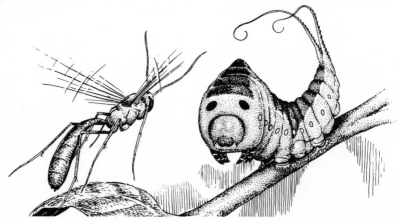

The puss moth caterpillar puffs up its front end and waves its 'tails' to frighten an enemy – one of the ichneumons (see p. 112).

easily on a branch of privet, especially when it has already eaten some of the leaves; but its bright green body is adorned with purple and white diagonal stripes which effectively break up its outline and cause it to 'disappear' amongst the foliage. The eyed hawkmoth caterpillar plays a similar game of hide-and-seek in the apple trees.

Gardens with sallows or poplars often harbour the amazing caterpillar of the puss moth, often brought to me in a jam jar and handed over at arm's length by terrified neighbours – children and adults alike. Up to 7 cm (nearly 3 inches) long, it can certainly put on a show of aggression when alarmed. The head is pulled into the front of the body, which swells and rears up like a face. At the same time two whip-like 'tails' are protruded from the rear and waved threateningly over the back. But it's all bluff: the caterpillar is harmless and is merely puffing itself up to frighten its enemies. At rest, its plump green body is very well camouflaged, with a dark brown 'saddle' on the back breaking up its outline and giving it the appearance of a rolled-up leaf.

Our garden trees and hedges support many twig-like caterpillars, including those of the peppered and swallowtailed moths, which can fool you with their rigid postures until you actually touch them. Presumably, the birds are fooled as well. On the other hand, a good number of moth caterpillars advertise themselves with bold colours, just like the large white butterfly larva (p. 66). These caterpillars possess nauseous flavours or irritating hairs, and the bold colours or patterns warn the birds to keep away. The effect is often enhanced by the caterpillars living in groups. The buff-tip is an excellent example. Writhing masses of the yellow and black caterpillars can be found on many trees, often defoliating whole branches in the summer, but the birds never touch them. The adult moth employs camouflage, however, resting on the ground and resembling a broken twig. Caterpillars of the lackey moth are equally destructive to trees. Dense clusters of the red, white and blue caterpillars can be found on large silken webs that they spin on the branches of many garden trees, especially plum, and also on hawthorn hedges. The latter also support the hairy larvae of the yellow-tail moth. Black, red and white, they show up clearly on the leaves, but only the cuckoo dares to eat them. Hairy caterpillars are regularly eaten by this bird, which seems immune to their irritation and gradually acquires a furry lining to its throat. Magpie moth caterpillars, avoided by most birds and even rejected by spiders, are also taken by the cuckoo, despite their bold warning colours of black and red on a creamy background. These caterpillars can be found on hawthorn and blackthorn hedges, and also on gooseberry and currant bushes in the garden, and the adults, which sport the same colours as their larvae, are common visitors to lights on summer evenings. My favourite among these flamboyant caterpillars, however, is that of the mullein moth, although I regularly lose a few flower spikes to it every year. White with a dense coating of black and yellow dots, the larvae sit brazenly on the mullein plants and munch through leaves and flower buds without a care in the world.

As we have already seen with the cabbage white caterpillars (p. 66), the warning colours have no effect on parasitic insects, nor does camouflage help against these attackers, which home in on the scents of their hosts. A high percentage of moth caterpillars are attacked by ichneumon flies (see p. 112) and also by parasitic relatives of the blow-flies. The grubs of these parasites grow up inside the caterpillars, and many moth collectors have been disappointed to find 'ugly' flies emerging from their pupae instead of the expected moths. Nevertheless, as long as you are prepared for such happenings, collecting caterpillars and feeding them in captivity is a good way of discovering what caterpillar turns into what moth: but you also need patience, for many species spend several months in the pupal state before emerging as adult moths.

Rearing caterpillars

Caterpillars of both butterflies and moths are easy to rear in captivity if you have plenty of the natural food plants. Suitable cages can be bought from dealers or made from round cake tins and sheets of clear plastic that can be formed into cylinders to fit the tins. The cages should be about 50 cm (20 inches) high and there should be small ventilation holes in the lids. Sprigs of food plant can be provided in small bottles of water — make sure the necks are plugged with tissue paper (not cotton wool, which can trap the caterpillars' tiny feet). Replace the food plant every day or two or as soon as it begins to look tired: caterpillars are used to completely fresh food in the wild. Large sweet jars and clear plastic boxes also make suitable caterpillar homes, but when using boxes you must put a layer of tissue in the bottom to absorb condensation. You don't need water for the food plant in these boxes. Plastic boxes are especially useful for very young caterpillars, but the tissue paper is even more important because the tiny larvae can be trapped in water droplets.

When fully grown, the caterpillars must be given somewhere to turn into pupae. Our garden butterflies will appreciate a few twigs to which they can attach themselves, whereas many moth larvae burrow into the ground to pupate. These species need a layer of peat or potting compost about 10 cm (4 inches) deep. Other moth larvae spin silken cocoons amongst the leaves of the food plant or amongst debris on the ground. Give them some twigs and some handfuls of dead leaves or wood shavings. Caterpillars that are about to pupate should be removed from the feeding cage and given a new home where they can go about their business undisturbed by younger caterpillars which are still feeding. You will know when they are ready to pupate because they wander ceaselessly around the cage as they search for suitable sites. Many also become somewhat darker. For guidance as to the conditions to provide, you can use a rough and ready rule of thumb: hairy moth caterpillars generally spin cocoons in leaves and debris, while hairless ones tend to burrow. But this is not an invariable rule.

Caterpillars that pupate in the autumn will usually remain as pupae throughout the winter and they must be put in a cool place. If left in the house they will either dry up and die or else they will develop quickly and emerge as adults in the winter, when there is no nectar for them and no mates. Keep them in a shed, but don't forget to look at them regularly as spring approaches. Make sure that the cages have plenty of twigs for the young insects to climb, and plenty of room for them to spread their wings. Release them in the garden when they start to fly.

Moths and light

It seems a bit daft for moths to wait until it's dark before they take to the air, and then to fly straight to the nearest street lamp or other light, but this is what happens with many moths – except that they don't actually fly straight. This paradoxical behaviour has long puzzled entomologists and there is no universally accepted explanation, although most biologists agree that it is connected with the moths' navigational system. It is believed that moths not actively seeking food or mates generally fly in straight lines by keeping their eyes at a fixed angle to the moon, which is the only major source of light at night in the wild. The insects will, however, use any other bright light for navigation, be it a street lamp or the entomologist's moth trap. Because these lights are relatively close, the moths have to keep adjusting their course to maintain the fixed angle between the light and their eyes. As a result, they gradually spiral towards the light and often crash into it. So, although moths certainly come to lights, it is perhaps more accurate to say that they are distracted by them than that they are attracted by them; the moths are not interested in the light in the way that many are interested in nectar and home in on the flowers. So why do so many stay and 'sunbathe' around the lights? The answer here is rather more simple: the poor things are fooled into thinking that morning has arrived and they settle down just as they do at day-break. The great majority of moths coming to light are males, for these are the moths that fly most, often emerging several days before the females and spreading themselves over the countryside before beginning the serious business of sex. Females don't fly much before mating, because they are heavily laden with eggs, and afterwards they are primarily concerned with sniffing out food plants on which to lay them.

Voracious lacewings

Shine a strong light through your window on a late summer evening and the window pane will soon be covered with delicate green insects with flimsy wings. These are the aptly-named lacewings, often called lacewing flies although they are not true flies (see p. 80). A metallic gleam in their eyes has earned these beautiful insects their alternative name of golden-eyes. There are several very similar species, with wings spanning between 20 and 40 mm ($\frac{3}{4}$ and $1\frac{1}{2}$ inches), and by day you can find them resting amongst the foliage of trees and shrubs and also in the herbaceous borders. When disturbed, they drift feebly away and soon come to rest again. They are

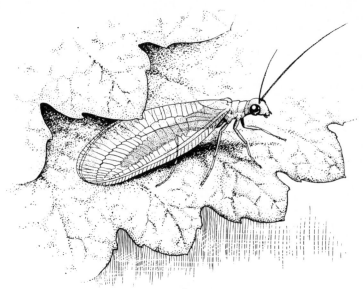

A green lacewing

good friends of the gardener, for each one will eat perhaps a thousand aphids in its lifetime of perhaps a couple of months. Some live much longer.

Lacewings lay their eggs under the leaves, with each egg hanging at the end of a slender thread. The egg-laying female makes the threads with quick-setting gum extruded from her rear end, and in some species the threads coalesce to form a stalk carrying perhaps a dozen eggs. The larvae that emerge from the eggs are brownish, shuttle-shaped creatures covered with bristles and, like the adults, they have phenomenal appetites for aphids. Whereas the adult lacewings literally chew up the aphids, however, the larvae simply drain them dry. Large curved jaws embrace and pierce the victim and, being hollow, enable the lacewing grub to suck out the juices. The empty aphid skin may be discarded when dry, but some lacewing species carefully fix their victims' skins to the spines on their backs as camouflage. A pile of rubbish crawling over a leaf is quite likely to be a lacewing larva in search of yet more victims.

The fully grown larva pupates in a silken case, usually in a rolled-up leaf or a bark crevice, and the pupa, equipped with legs and jaws, bites its way out of the cocoon and may wander some distance before settling down for the adult to emerge. Most species pass the winter as larvae and pupate in the spring, but one very common one hibernates as an adult. This is *Chrysoperla carnea*, which assumes a flesh colour in the autumn and very often enters houses and other buildings to look for cosy hibernation sites. Most lacewings have two or three generations in a year.

The true flies

Many insects have the word fly in their names, for obvious reasons: dragonfly, butterfly, caddis fly and scorpion fly are familiar examples. But these are not flies in the strict sense. True flies include things like house-flies, bluebottles, hover-flies, mosquitoes and crane-flies. They differ from most other insects in having just one pair of wings, but their flight is in no way impaired – as you will know if you have ever watched the hovering and darting flight of the hover-fly or the speed with which a house-fly evades the approaching swatter. The hind wings have been converted into tiny pin-like organs known as halteres or balancers, which help the fly to maintain a steady course without rolling. Without its halteres, the fly becomes at best very clumsy and usually can't fly at all. The halteres are easily seen in the crane-flies and their slender-bodied relatives, but in the stouter flies they are covered by membranes.

The hover-fly Episyrphus balteatus *often produces dense swarms in the garden in summer.*

The true flies are an immense group, with more than 5,000 British species and a very wide range of form. The great majority are active by day. All take liquid food, although some hover-flies can crush pollen grains and eat them, and most species feed on nectar. There are, however, many species with less attractive habits, including those that lap putrid liquids from dung and carrion and those that have acquired a taste for blood. There is a correspondingly wide range of feeding apparatus, including the mop-like tongues of the house-fly and bluebottle and the hypodermic needles of the mosquitoes and other blood-suckers.

Fly larvae are all legless, but still immensely variable in form and habit. It's difficult to realize that the sturdy leatherjackets nibbling away at roots in the soil (see p. 84) belong to the same major group of insects as the mosquito grubs that swim jerkily in your water butt and the slug-like hover-fly grubs gobbling up the aphids on your roses, but all eventually give rise to true flies. Many fly larvae pupate in barrel-shaped cases. The hover-flies are generally the most noticeable flies in the garden during the summer. Most of them are quite large and brightly coloured, and they tend to sit conspicuously in the flowers – often in large numbers. Many bear striking resemblances to bees and wasps (see p. 108), but if you look closely you will see that there are just two wings as opposed to four wings in bees and wasps. In addition, the hover-flies have larger eyes and smaller antennae than the wasps. When busy feeding, they'll often let you get near enough to see the hover-fly hall-mark – the false margin formed by veins running just inside the outer margin of the wing. The insects are well named, for many hover almost motionless in shafts of sunlight, seemingly enjoying their sun-bathing, for they quickly return to their chosen spots after disturbance. Many emit a soft whine as they hover, the pitch varying from species to species – suggesting that the sound is used to bring the sexes together for mating.

The drone-fly, named for its uncanny resemblance to a male honey-bee, is one of our commonest hover-flies and can be seen at all times of the year, even in the depths of winter. The adults sleep fitfully in sheds and other buildings during the colder months, waking to bask on sunny walls whenever the air temperature gets to about 5°C. They are among the first flies at the crocuses and other spring flowers and, together with several close relatives, they are abundant again in the autumn – when the males often hold territories and dart aggressively at other flies hoping to share their flowers. In common with most other hover-flies, they play a major role in pollinating our flowers. The drone-fly larva, by comparison, is a rather dirty beast, feeding on decaying matter in muddy ponds and ditches. It is known as the rat-tailed maggot, for it has a telescopic breathing tube at the hind end. Up to about 15 cm (6 inches) long, this tube can draw air from the

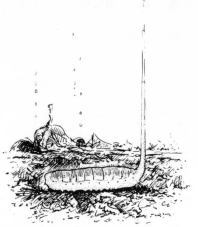

The rat-tailed maggot taking a breather with its telescopic breathing tube.

surface while the larva itself remains concealed in the mud and debris.

Many hover-fly larvae, including about half of the British species, feed on aphids. Generally pale with green or brown markings, they taper strongly towards the front and are remarkably agile for legless maggots. They plough their way through aphid colonies at a very useful rate, each destroying perhaps 250 aphids during its life. Their pear-shaped pupal cases can be seen attached to the leaves around the aphid colonies. A few hover-flies are harmful, none more so in the garden than the large bulb-fly or narcissus-fly (*Merodon equestris*). The furry adults have several colour forms and they mimic several different bumble bees as they bask on the ground or on the dying leaves of daffodils in late spring. Eggs are laid in late spring on the leaves and the grubs burrow into the bulbs, which they gradually destroy during the ensuing months.

The bee-fly, a harmless mimic of bumble bees.

The long rigid tongue of the bee-fly is a wicked-looking implement and understandably causes some alarm when the insect is seen for the first time – often hovering close to the gardener on sunny spring days. But it is a harmless creature, using its tongue only to probe for nectar. A good bumble bee mimic (see p. 108) with a furry brown coat, it is common at aubretia and other spring flowers and also spends a lot of time simply hovering over or resting on a sunny patch of soil. Although it resembles the hover-flies in flight, it is only distantly related to them. Its larvae live as parasites of the grubs of solitary bees (see p. 99). The female bee-fly generally scatters her eggs while hovering over the bees' nests, and the resulting larvae enter the nests and attach themselves to the bee grubs.

Leafy umbrellas

A number of small flies, notably the winter gnats, fly in damp weather and even in light rain. Male winter moths also drift about on wet nights, but most of our insects dislike rain and seek shelter as soon as it starts. The butterflies and other sun-loving insects don't even hang about that long: they're off for cover as soon as the clouds roll up and hide the sun, and they're safely tucked up well before the rain begins. Although some insects have water-repellent hairs or waxes on their wings, they can't stand up to heavy rain. A direct hit may send an insect crashing to the ground and render it unable to fly for some time – and thus easy prey for various enemies. If you've ever rescued a fly from the garden pond you'll know that it takes some time for its wings to dry and become airworthy again. Any sort of overhang may be used for shelter, with leaves, not surprisingly, the commonest choice. They make super umbrellas for many kinds of insects, and even quite large butterflies can 'disappear' when they settle down under the leaves and bring their wings tightly together. Insects also take cover from wind, which can blow them far from home and cause many to perish.

Gangling crane-flies

People dislike the large crane-flies or daddy-long-legs almost as much as they hate spiders, which suggests that the long legs have something to do with the dislike (see p. 116), for this is the only similarity between the two groups. The insects fly into the house in the evenings, especially in late

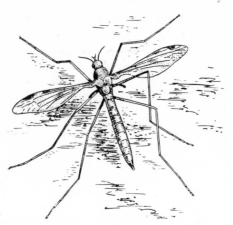

Unlike most flies, the large crane-flies rest with their wings outstretched.

summer, and then struggle frantically up walls and windows with their legs splaying in all directions. One or more legs may be lost in the process, but the flies are not too bothered – they can stand on three legs if necessary. The invaders belong to two main species, both greyish brown and difficult to separate. Males have swollen rear ends, while the females taper to a point which is used to shove their eggs into the soil. Their larvae are the destructive leatherjackets – squelchy grey grubs that grow fat on a diet of roots. They prefer grassy places and most of the adults that come into the house have grown up under the lawn or in nearby fields or roadsides. They can be a real problem when rough, grassy areas are converted to vegetable plots, chewing through the roots of the freshly planted vegetables and also coming to the surface to nibble right through the bases of the stems (see also p. 70). Damage is greatest in the spring, when the vegetables are small and the leatherjackets are at their biggest.

Gnats and midges

Gnat is an old English name for the mosquito, but today it is commonly used for a wide range of small, slender flies, especially those that do not bite. Midge is usually commonly used for small flies, both biting and non-biting forms, and we have to qualify the names to give them any clear meaning. Winter gnats are the small flies that we most commonly see dancing up and down in compact swarms on damp afternoons in late autumn and winter, usually stationing themselves over some prominent landmark that keeps hem together. My car is regularly used as such an assembly point. Most of he dancers are males and the performance attracts the females, but as soon s the latter arrive they are generally waltzed off for other purposes. This ersion of Saturday night at the Palais is quite common among insects (see . 111). Winter gnats are particularly common in woods, where their larvae eed on decaying leaves, but they are also plentiful in gardens with hedges nd compost heaps to keep the grubs happy.

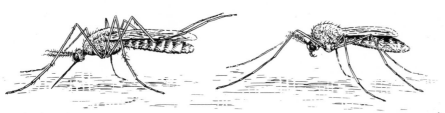

The female mosquito (left) *takes blood with her needle-like mouth-parts. The chironomid* (right) *is similar, but has shorter wings and no blood-sucking apparatus.*

Amongst the numerous midges in your garden, the most abundant are ikely to be the various species of chironomids or non-biting midges – specially if you have a pond or water butt in which they can spend their arly stages. The aquatic larvae of many species are bright red and known as loodworms. Adults can often be seen resting on walls near the water. They esemble mosquitoes, but they hold their wings roofwise over the body nstead of flat, and a good deal of the rear end pokes out beyond the wings. The males, recognized by their bushy antennae, often swarm like winter nats. As the name indicates, these midges are not blood-suckers. You night collect a few mosquito bites in the garden, and the culprit is likely to e Britain's largest mosquito, *Culiseta annulata*, with prominent white ands on the abdomen and legs. It often breeds in garden ponds and in tagnant rainwater butts. But you have nothing to fear from our com-nonest mosquito, *Culex pipiens*. This also breeds in water butts, and it ommonly hibernates in the house, but it prefers birds to people and the vorst it is likely to do to you is keep you awake as it whines around the edroom looking for a way out.

The fungus and the fly

Towards the end of summer, especially n a damp season, many gardeners find atches of plants clothed with small dark flies. Close inspection shows that, although clinging to the foliage in a life-like attitude, the flies are all dead;

and an even closer look reveals the cause of death – a fungus oozing in furry blobs from the flies' abdomens. Fungal spores are picked up on the body and the tiny threads emerging from the spores get into the insect through its breathing pores. Multiplying rapidly inside the body, they soon cause the insect to become lethargic and it settles down to die. Probably the commonest garden fly afflicted in this way is the cabbage root-fly, whose larvae stunt your brassicas by tunnelling in their roots. For some unexplained reason, the dying flies are attracted to each other and their 'graveyards' may cover a considerable area. Every leaf of every parsnip plant in a 5-metre row was

blackened by these fly corpses in my own garden a few years ago, although the neighbouring broccoli plants were untouched. I have also seen several metres of hedgerow clothed with flies which had met an untimely end after emerging from the neighbouring rape crop.

But it's not just the cabbage root-fly that suffers from fungal attack. Many hover-flies can be seen clinging to grass heads in a life-like death, while your window panes may be the final resting places of mouldy house-flies. A close look at the latter will probably show a white halo of spores around it – just waiting to be picked up by another fly.

Graveyard for flies.

My favourite fly

A radio interviewer once asked me to name my favourite fly and I had no hesitation in singing the praises of the stilt-legged fly, although I doubt if many listeners knew what I was on about. The fly is usually quite common in my own garden in early summer, but I have seen it in very few other gardens and generally meet it on rank herbage close to water. It's about as thick as a pin and no more than about 6 mm (¼ inch) long and, true to its name, it stands on six very long and slender legs. In hours of watching, spread over several years, I have only once seen a stilt-legged fly attempt to eat anything – an aphid which it obviously didn't fancy, for it was abandoned within seconds – but I never tire of watching the insects striding slowly and somewhat awkwardly over the leaves and scuttling rather more rapidly round to the underside when they feel I am getting too close. Chacun à son goût!

The aptly named stilt-legged fly.

An abundance of beetles

There are more kinds of beetle than of any other type of animal: over 250,000 in the world, with some 20,000 of them living in Europe. Nearly 4,000 live in Britain. The group includes the bulkiest of all insects and also some of the smallest, and yet they are remarkably uniform in their construction. All have biting jaws, and with few exceptions they all have tough, horny front wings known as elytra. The hind wings, when present, are flimsy and folded under the elytra when not in use for flying. There is also a tough plate known as the pronotum just behind the head. Beetles live virtually everywhere on land and in fresh water, and they feed on just about everything they can chew. Many are plant-eating pests, while others are predators or scavengers. The garden contains a good sprinkling of all three types. All begin life as eggs and pass through both larval and pupal stages as they grow up, the larvae varying a great deal according to their habitats and types of food. Many share the adult food, while others have a totally different diet.

Prowling ground beetles

Unless you are a nocturnal prowler yourself, you are most likely to meet the ground beetles when lifting logs or large stones in the garden, or perhaps when moving boxes in the shed, for these largely predatory beetles sleep under such objects by day. But they are light sleepers, and when you disturb them they are likely to scamper rapidly away, giving you little chance to examine them. If you want a close look, try setting a few pitfall traps around the garden, as shown in the illustration. The beetles readily oblige by falling

A simple pitfall trap. Sink two plastic cups, one inside the other, so that the top rim is flush with the soil surface. You can lift out the inner cup to examine your catch without the pit collapsing. The cover is not essential, but does keep out rain and mice.

in during the night. There are many different species, mostly dark and rather angular beetles with long legs and antennae. Few of them fly and the majority don't even have any hind wings. Even the elytra are often fused together, giving greater protection to the body on and under the ground. The insects hunt mainly on the ground, but also climb trees and other plants in search of prey. They are very fond of slugs in the garden, and therefore useful creatures to have around. They find their prey partly by scent and partly by detecting sounds and other vibrations, but the majority are not averse to supplementing their meat with fruit and vegetables as well. Some actually prefer vegetable food.

Among the commonest of our garden ground beetles is the shiny black *Pterostichus madidus*, distinguished from most of its fellows by its chestnut-coloured legs. This is certainly the most numerous species in garden pitfall traps and it is one of those that likes fruit. It is often known as the strawberry beetle because of its regular looting of this crop. Much more striking, however, is the violet ground beetle, with a beautiful violet sheen

A ground beetle with a juicy caterpillar. Ground beetles destroy lots of garden pests.

on the pronotum and around the margins of its black elytra. The closely related *Carabus nemoralis* is very similar, except that its elytra are metallic green or bronze.

The devil's coach-horse or cock-tail beetle, a jet black insect some 20–30 mm (⁴/₅ to 1¹/₅ inches) long, can be found in the same places as the ground beetles. I regularly find it under flower-pots in my greenhouse – where it is a welcome nocturnal predator of slugs and other destructive creepy-crawlies – and also in the compost heap. It is one of the very large group known as rove beetles, in which the elytra are very short and leave the abdomen uncovered. Many members of the group are mistaken for earwigs, although they have no pincers. They are scavengers and predators, often associated with carrion and other decaying matter. The devil's coach-horse gets its alternative name of cock-tail because, when alarmed, it turns towards its attacker and raises its rear end. At the same time it opens its huge jaws in a threatening attitude and releases a pungent secretion from the abdomen. Legend has it that the devil's curse, or even death, comes to the beholder of this spectacle. It's frightening when seen for the first time, and the beetle can certainly nip, but it's otherwise harmless – unless you're a slug or some other small invertebrate.

The bumbling cockchafer

If you live in a wooded area you've probably met the cockchafer or maybug crashing into lighted windows with a loud thud in the evenings. Known as the maybug because it normally appears in May, it is a reddish brown beetle about 2½ cm (an inch) long and with a sharply pointed rear. The male has enormous fan-like antennae with which he sniffs out the female. Both sexes fly noisily through the night in search of tender shoots on a wide range of trees and shrubs and, when abundant, they can strip a sizeable tree of its leaves overnight. The insects are right pests in the larval stage as well, for their fat white grubs feed on the roots of many kinds of plants and are especially damaging to cereals and other grasses. The adults, especially the males, are attracted to light in much the same way as moths (see p. 78) and are often abundant in the moth-collector's light trap.

Colourful ladybirds

Known as 'beasts of the good lord' in France and 'Mary's beetles' in Germany, the brightly coloured ladybirds have a long, but unexplained connection with religion in many countries and are commonly believed to bring good fortune when they land on people. They are certainly beneficial in the garden, but their popularity does not depend on our knowing just how many aphids they eat. Nursery rhymes encourage children to make friends with the ladybird long before they ever discover anything of its habits.

Several species live in our gardens, nearly all helping in the fight against aphids. If you're troubled by these pests it's worth hunting for a few ladybirds and installing them on your plants (they'll also help the fight against pests on houseplants). They'll munch their way through several dozen in a single day. Largest and commonest is the 7-spot ladybird, with seven black spots on its bright red elytra. It lays batches of yellow, skittle-shaped eggs on aphid-infested plants, and the resulting slate-blue larvae join the adults at the feast. Each larva will demolish several hundred aphids during its 3-week development, and then it attaches itself to a leaf and turns into a pupa – with no protection other than a strong resemblance to a bird's dropping. During the summer the whole development from egg to adult may be completed in a month.

The 2-spot ladybird is somewhat smaller and normally bears just two black spots on its red elytra. It is a remarkably variable creature, though, and often turns up with black elytra and red spots. This form is especially common in northern areas, where temperatures are lower and sunshine is less frequent. It has an advantage over the normal red form because the dark elytra absorb heat more efficiently in the cooler climate. Although red and black are the commonest colours for ladybirds, there are also a number of yellow and black species, including the very small 22-spot ladybird which has eleven small black spots on each yellow elytron and a further five on the pronotum just behind the head. It is commonly found on gooseberries and other garden shrubs, although absent from Scottish gardens. It feeds mainly on the mildews growing on the leaves and twigs and pays little attention to aphids.

The bold colours of the adult ladybirds are warning colours, advertising the beetles' unpleasant taste and warning birds to keep away (see p. 66). If you handle a ladybird roughly, or confine it in your hand for a short while, it will exude a drop of pungent fluid which will stain your hand and continue to smell for quite a while. Any bird ignoring the warning gets a beakful of this fluid and doesn't usually make the same mistake again.

In the autumn or winter you might come across a mass of ladybirds in a sheltered spot. Several species go in for this mass hibernation, probably drawn together by their strong scent. They often bed down under loose bark, but I have also found sleeping colonies under piles of newspaper in the shed, in a box of old clothes in the loft, and even in the narrow gap around an ill-fitting window. The insects often use the same site year after year, although they are obviously not the same individuals, since a year is about the longest they live: the scent lingers in the hibernation sites from year to year and attracts fresh ladybirds each autumn.

Woodworm:
the unseen menace indoors and out

Few houses can be lucky enough to escape the attention of the woodworm at some time or other. It was once found mainly in older buildings, but with the increased use of the more palatable softwoods since the war it has become a serious pest. Surveys a few years ago revealed that over 80% of our houses were infested with woodworm. Modern timber treatments can reduce the amount of damage done, but the insect remains a serious threat to the householder. The woodworm is not a worm at all: it is the larva of a small brown beetle, usually known as a furniture beetle, although its New Zealand name of common house borer is much more appropriate because it attacks far more than furniture. Floorboards, doors and roof timbers all suffer, and the worst feature is that the damage goes on unseen inside the wood. The grubs munch their way through the timber for up to three years, but it is not until the mature beetles chew their way out through the familiar worm holes that we notice the problem. And by then a great deal of damage may have been done. Solid beams can be reduced to dust, boxed in by just a wafer-thin shell of timber, and chair legs can collapse without warning when they reach this stage – I speak from painful experience. The adult beetles, the size of a small grain of rice, can be found at any time of year indoors, although they emerge mainly in June and July and can then be seen crawling on the window panes in an attempt to get out. Most of the beetles seen here, however, are males. The insects mate very soon after emerging from the timber and the females devote most of their time to egg-laying – often going back into the larval tunnels for this purpose, although they will lay in any small crack or crevice in the woodwork.

It is not just indoors that we have to contend with the woodworm. It was chewing its way through timber long before we started to build houses, and a large population continues to live out of doors – probably far larger than lives in our buildings. These woodworm play a major role in the breakdown of dead trees in the wild, but unfortunately they can't distinguish between these and our sheds and fences. Almost any untreated garden timber more than about ten years old is likely to show signs of woodworm, and when the adult beetles have left you might well find tiny solitary bees (see p. 99) nesting in the abandoned holes. The woodworm grubs usually develop more rapidly out of doors because the timber is damp and often contaminated by fungi, making it more palatable to the insects.

Click goes the beetle

Click beetles are shuttle-shaped insects, usually dingy brown, with an amusing party trick. If placed on their backs – a rather dodgy position for many beetles – they can right themselves by leaping into the air. It's easy to watch the action by putting a beetle on the table or in the palm of your hand, but it's not so easy to see exactly what happens. The beetle arches its back along the mobile joint at the rear of the pronotum, and holds this position momentarily by means of a tiny peg resting on a ridge on the underside of the body. Tension builds up in the body muscles, overcomes the friction holding the peg in place, and causes the peg to slip suddenly over the ridge. The body then bends very rapidly in the opposite direction, with a loud click and with sufficient force to throw the beetle into the air. From a hard surface it may leap to a height of 30 cm (12 inches), and while airborne it will somersault several times. It doesn't always land the right way up, but it goes on trying until it does.

Adult click beetles might be fun to watch, but their larvae are not fun to have in the garden. They are the destructive wireworms – tough, yellowish worm-like grubs with three pairs of short legs at the front. They take several years to mature, during which time they play havoc with the roots of many kinds of plants. They also attack seeds, and if your runner beans fail to show you could well find that the buried seeds have been hollowed out by these pests.

A click beetle and (right) *its destructive larva – the wireworm.*

The Colorado beetle – an unwelcome alien

Until potatoes arrived in North America in the middle of the 19th century the Colorado beetle was just an ordinary insect, offending nobody as it nibbled its way through the wild nightshades. But it found the

An established alien – the Colorado beetle.

introduced potato plants much to its liking and soon became a pest. Within a few years it had spread to most potato-growing regions of North America and was looking out across the Atlantic. Stowaways managed to cross to Europe on the shipping routes, and by 1920 the pest was firmly established in southern Europe. Today it is found in most parts of Europe and causes severe losses to potato growers, although modern insecticides can keep it under control. Living in Belgium just after the war, I well remember the evening beetle hunts: I was given a bucket and, to shouts of 'Allez, cherchez les doryphores,' I went out to the fields. It was not difficult to fill a bucket with the beetles and their plump pink larvae before supper. Unchecked, the insects chew the stems and leaves of the plants, reducing them to smelly black stumps and causing total loss of the crop. Constant vigilance by the authorities has prevented the beetle from establishing itself in Britain, although individual beetles commonly arrive with produce from the Continent. Any discovery in Britain must be notified to the police or the Ministry of Agriculture immediately. Establishment of the pest in Britain could be much more serious than it is on the Continent because of our later growing season: new adults emerging in late summer would find plenty of potatoes still in the fields and gardens and would be able to feed up before hibernating in the soil. The earlier lifting of potatoes on the Continent denies the beetles this last supper and many fail to survive the winter.

Felonious flea beetles

Anyone who grows brassicas from seed will recognize the work of the flea beetles – neat round holes in the seedling leaves, sometimes so numerous that the little plants just give up and die. The beetles are only 2–3 mm long and generally have dark, shiny elytra. Like the fleas after which they are named, they are great jumpers, and if you examine your seedlings closely

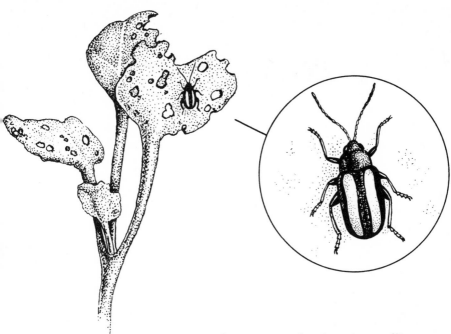

A flea beetle and the characteristic damage caused to brassica seedlings.

you will see the beetles leaping many times their own length. Many people do actually mistake them for fleas. Several species attack our brassicas, one of the commonest being *Phyllotreta nemorum*. Commonly known as the large striped flea beetle, this insect has a yellow stripe on each elytron. It is also known as the turnip flea, for it is especially fond of turnip and radish seedlings. Flea beetles hibernate amongst dead leaves and other garden debris and wake with the spring sunshine. If there are no succulent seedlings to nibble, they are quite happy to feed on mature cabbages and other plants that have stood through the winter. Eggs are laid in the soil, and the larvae continue the attack on the brassicas. Most larvae feed on the roots, but those of the turnip flea tunnel in the young leaves. A new generation of adults emerges in late summer, but little damage is done at this time because the plants are well grown and can shrug off the effects of even quite a lot of small beetles. There is also a potato flea beetle, a yellowish brown species producing conspicuous round holes in potato leaves in the spring and again in the autumn if the potatoes have not been lifted. Its grubs feed on the roots. The species is also abundant on the related bittersweet or woody nightshade.

Nosey weevils

The weevils are a very large group of beetles, recognized by the possession of a distinct snout at the front of the head. The jaws are carried at the tip of the snout and the antennae are attached somewhere along its length. Mostly rather small insects, weevils are almost all vegetarians and their legless grubs generally feed inside their plant hosts. If you've been generous enough to leave a bed of nettles for the butterflies (see p. 66), you will undoubtedly find plenty of weevils in it — especially greenish ones with a golden sheen. The colour is produced by a coating of tiny scales, such as is found in many weevils. In the absence of nettles, however, one of the commonest garden weevils is *Sitona lineatus*, commonly known as the pea weevil. One of several similar species, it is about 5 mm ($1/5$ inch) long and dull brown in colour. It is often found sunning itself on paths and walls, especially in the spring after waking from hibernation in the hedge bottom or amongst other rough vegetation or debris. If disturbed, it simply falls to the ground, pulls its legs and antennae tightly against its body, and pretends to be a seed. The beetles feed on broad beans and clovers as well as peas, nibbling semi-circular chunks out of the leaf edges to leave them scalloped just like postage stamps. Seedlings may be seriously retarded by such an attack, but older plants are not usually harmed, even when every leaf is affected. Eggs are laid in the soil in late spring and the grubs feed inside the root nodules which are characteristic of all members of the pea family. New adults emerge later in the summer and add more perforations to the leaves before flying off to find hibernation sites. They often get into the house at this time, much to the consternation of the householder who assumes they are bent on destroying the house: apart from the snout, which isn't terribly obvious in *Sitona*, the insects are not that different from furniture beetles (see p. 92) in appearance. I once had a visit from a gentleman who was sweeping the beetles up by the handful and fighting a losing battle. It turned out that his house faced 20 acres of field beans, which were drying rapidly and causing the beetles to fly off in their thousands. I recommended nothing more than a vacuum cleaner.

Some weevils will live permanently in the house if they get the chance. These are the species that live on grain and assorted cereal products. The common grain weevil is a slender, dark brown insect about 3 mm long and it is a serious pest in granaries. You are most likely to find it in the house if you live near a granary or if you keep grain for feeding poultry. Similar weevils can be found in other dried foods, including nuts as well as cereal products, and were well known to the sailors of yesteryear through infesting their biscuit rations, but modern hygiene and packaging have greatly reduced the weevil problem today.

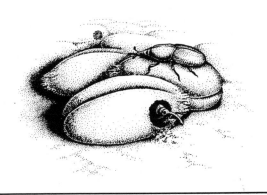

Was it a wasp – or wasn't it?

The wasp beetle is an excellent wasp mimic (see p. 108), despite having no membranous wings on show. The mimicry depends as much on the beetle's behaviour as on its appearance, for it scuttles over the vegetation like a wasp and takes off with a buzz as well. Many people are convinced that they've seen a wasp, and birds are fooled too.

The deceptive wasp beetle, a harmless mimic.

Garden bees

The first bees to buzz around your garden in the spring are usually large furry bumble bees, woken from hibernation by the first sunny spell – often as early as February. There are several different kinds, generally easy to recognize by their colours. The red-tailed bumble bee is jet black with a brick-red rear; the buff-tailed and white-tailed species are both black with yellow bands and either a buff or a white rear; and the carder bee is largely brown with a good deal of black showing through the hairs. These and several other species probe the early flowers for nectar, but collect no pollen at this stage: pollen is mainly the food of the youngsters, whereas the adults mainly drink nectar. They will not begin nesting for some time.

Clockwise from top left: *red-tailed bumble bee; buff-tailed bumble bee feeding in white deadnettle flower; honey bee with bulging pollen baskets.*

The honey bee is not far behind the bumble bees in the spring and is a common visitor to the early crocuses. Slimmer and less hairy than the bumble bees, it collects both pollen and nectar right away, for it lives in perennial colonies and it is never too early to start replenishing the larder. Large blobs of pollen are clearly visible on the hind legs as the bees buzz from flower to flower. The pollen is stored in the combs of the nest and used mainly to feed the bees' grubs.

There are also many solitary bees in the garden. These do not live in colonies like the bumble bees (p. 101) and honey bees. Each female makes a small nest which she stocks with pollen and nectar and in which she lays a few eggs. She then seals it up and leaves the resulting grubs to feed themselves on the stored food. The mother usually dies long before her offspring mature – which is often not until the following year. Solitary bees are particularly common in the spring, when they play an important role in pollinating our fruit trees and bushes. You will also find them busying themselves at dandelion flowers, although many are small enough to burrow out of sight amongst the tightly packed florets. One of the most conspicuous garden species is the tawny mining bee (*Andrena fulva*), whose female, resplendent in her fox-red fur coat, forages among our currant and gooseberry blossoms. She is known as a mining bee because, in common with many of her cousins, she excavates her nest in the ground. You will often see her at work on the lawn, where her nest entrance may be surrounded by a conical mound of excavated soil. Many miners nest in dead wood and in walls, either digging tunnels themselves or using existing cavities. The little harebell carpenter bee, so called for its liking for harebells and other campanulas, can even squeeze itself into the flight holes of the furniture beetle (see p. 92), although it has no room to turn round in the tunnels.

It is possible to encourage the solitary bees to nest in the garden by providing them with suitable nesting sites. Set aside a few logs in which they can build, and encourage them even further by drilling holes of various diameters up to about 8 mm (⅓ inch): the bees will be happy to move in. Stand the logs where you can watch the comings and goings of the bees – laden with pollen on their legs or abdomens when they fly in but neat and tidy when they emerge again. Drill a few holes in an old wall as well, and if you have to build any kind of wall in the garden incorporate a few patches of soft mortar to encourage the mason bees and those species that normally mine in sandy soil. Bundles of short, hollow canes or even drinking straws glued under window sills also make attractive homes for the solitary bees, but make sure that one end of each tube is closed.

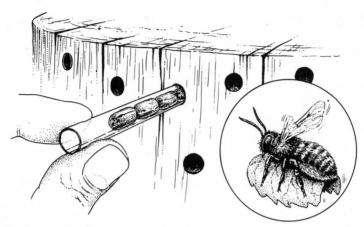

The leaf-cutter bee bringing a leaf section to her nest. Her sausage-shaped nest cells can be seen if you can persuade her to build in a glass tube set in a hole in a log.

One of the most interesting of the solitary bees, although rose growers might not agree, is the leaf-cutter bee. This is the insect responsible for the neat semi-circles cut from our rose leaves, and sometimes from the petals as well. The female, easily identified by the bright orange pollen brush on her underside, cuts the leaf with her jaws and then flies off to her burrow with the cut section neatly rolled under her body. The leaf segments are used to make a string of short, sausage-shaped cells, each of which receives an egg and a supply of food. The burrow is generally excavated in dead wood, but the bee will use all kinds of narrow cavities, including any hollow canes that you care to provide.

The sting

Bees and wasps and many ants possess stings, usually tucked away inside the rear end of the body and brought out when needed. The sting is actually a modified ovipositor or egg-layer, and is therefore found only in females. It is connected to a bag of venom inside the abdomen, and it is this venom that causes the pain when you are stung. The venom is a complex mixture of proteins and other materials, including histamine, and its exact composition varies from insect to insect. The solitary wasps use their stings to paralyse their victims prior to storing them in their nests (see p. 109), while the other stinging insects use their stings primarily for defence. They will not normally attack unless they feel they or their nests are being threatened. Most stings are dished out when people get in front of a nest and obstruct the passage of the insects. The honey bee sting is strongly barbed and is not easily withdrawn from human skin. Having stung you, the bee can normally get away only by tearing herself free and leaving the sting and venom sac behind, which is fatal for her, but it's all part of her job as a worker in the colony. If you are unlucky enough to be stung, don't grab the venom sac, for this will merely pump more venom into you: try to scrape the sting out without exerting any pressure on the sac.

A swarm of bees

Only the honey bee forms true swarms. Swarming is a way of producing new colonies and it normally occurs when the population of a hive gets too big. The queen flies out with a dense cloud of workers, whose job will be to establish the new colony. The flying swarm certainly looks menacing, but it is harmless: the workers are so full of honey that they would find it difficult to bend their bodies and jab in their stings. Shortly after leaving the hive, the swarm settles on a tree and remains there in a dense cluster while the workers decide where to build their new nest. This is the time for the bee-keeper to capture the swarm and instal it in one of his hives, but many swarms get away. Some of the workers would have been scouting around for new homes even before the swarm left the hive, and now they have another look. Returning to the swarm, the scouts 'dance' excitedly over the surface and persuade other workers to go and look at what they've found. The speed and direction of the dance tell the other bees where to go, and if they like what they see they will also dance when they return to the swarm. The scouts may suggest several different sites to start with, but eventually they all agree on one site and all perform the same dance. This is the signal for the swarm to move off to the chosen site, which is often in a hollow tree although it may be anywhere that offers sufficient shelter; sometimes the bees will choose an empty hive of their own accord. The workers then get busy with the construction of new combs. Meanwhile, the workers left in the old hive have reared a new queen to ensure that the old colony continues.

The bumble bee colony

The furry bumble bees that lumber around our gardens in early spring are all queens, and virtually all of them will have mated during the previous summer. It's hard luck on those that didn't, for there are no males around now. The mated queens gradually turn their attention to nesting as more flowers open to provide pollen and nectar. Most of them choose underground sites for their nests, often selecting old mouse holes in well drained banks, although some species nest amongst long grass on the surface. The nest consists of shredded grass and other vegetation, inside which the queen lays a few eggs on a cake of pollen. The resulting grubs feed on the pollen at first, but they grow quickly and mother is soon fully occupied in bringing in fresh supplies of both pollen and nectar. She can carry more than half her own weight of pollen on her hind legs and defies all the laws of aerodynamics as she flies back to the nest with it. In fact, the aeronautical engineers tell us that bumble bees shouldn't be able to fly at all with their heavy bodies and small wings – but the bees don't know that.

The first grubs are soon ready to pupate in papery cocoons, and while they are safely tucked up the queen gets on with feeding a second batch of grubs and laying further eggs. The first new adults emerge about a month after the first eggs were laid. They are all workers – sterile females – and very much smaller than the queen. You can be forgiven for thinking that they belong to a different species when they start flying around the garden. They relieve their mother of all foraging work, but she continues to work in the nest for the rest of the spring and summer, building wax cells for further egg batches and also helping to feed the young grubs with pollen and nectar which the workers store in their old cocoons. As the colony builds up its numbers, more and more food is brought in and the later grubs get a better deal. Later workers are thus somewhat larger than the early batches, and towards the end of the season the grubs receive so much food that they develop into plump new queens, with functional sex organs. Males are produced at about the same time from unfertilized eggs – the normal procedure for producing males among the bees and wasps and their relatives – and these mate with the new queens. The latter then seek hibernation sites in the soil and the old colonies disintegrate. Some males and workers may linger on until the autumn frosts, but most bumble bees have disappeared from our gardens by the end of the summer.

Cuckoo in the nest

Most of our garden bumble-bee species are put upon by 'lazy' relatives with no worker caste and no pollen-collecting equipment of their own. For obvious reasons, these scroungers are called cuckoo bees. The females, protected by tougher coats and superior stinging power, invade the bumble bee nests when not too many workers have been reared, and after a bit of a scuffle they are tolerated. They then start to lay their eggs, and the bumble bee workers rear the alien grubs along with their own brothers and sisters. The bumble bee queen is usually killed before long and the whole colony dies out – but not before a new generation of cuckoo bees has been successfully reared. The cuckoo bees are generally very similar to their host species, which presumably allows them to approach the nests without too much trouble, but they are less hairy and their wings are usually a little darker.

The thieving bumble bee

Adult bees feed mainly on energy-rich nectar, which they suck from the flowers with their tubular tongues. In the normal course of events, they pay for the nectar by pollinating the flowers, but some bumble bees have discovered a way of pinching nectar without pollinating the flowers. Instead of going in through the front door, the bee bites a hole in the base of the flower to get at the nectar. These thieving bumble bees are mainly the white-tailed and buff-tailed species, whose tongues are relatively short – about 10 mm (²/₅ inch) long. They usually attack only the deeper-throated flowers, whose nectar they cannot reach in the legitimate way. Runner bean flowers are commonly robbed by the bees, although this does not prevent pollination by other insects. In fact, it might actually help, by allowing smaller insects to crawl into the flowers and do the job.

A buff-tailed bumble bee biting a hole in a comfrey flower to steal the nectar which it can't reach by the normal route.

Sugar-loving wasps

Most parties have their gate-crashers, and a summer garden party often gets more than its fair share – dozens of wasps intent on stuffing themselves with anything from the trifle to the cucumber sandwiches and washing it down with any booze that's going. The party may take on the appearance of a tick-tack convention, with arms being waved in all directions to ward off the wasps – usually to no avail. In fact, arm-waving is one of the best ways of attracting the wasps and getting stung. Ignoring them is much better, although much more difficult; they'll still eat your food, but they're unlikely to sting. You can try luring them away with a bowl of fruit, liberally doused with beer or wine, at the other side of the garden. Granny, of course, would have used a jam-jar, well baited with jam and half-filled with water to drown the insects.

But wasps have their interesting and even useful side. The normal visitors to our meal tables are social wasps which, like the bumble bees, live in populous colonies each ruled by a queen. A few males are produced in the summer, but otherwise the colony members are all female workers. As with the bumble bees, the colony lasts for just one season, with only young mated queens surviving the winter. They hide themselves away in log piles, sheds, attics and even cupboards full of clothes, after gorging themselves on nectar from ivy and other late-flowering plants. Waking in the spring, the queens feast on whatever nectar is available, with the flowers of currants and cotoneasters being particular favourites. The next job is to find somewhere to start a nest, and for most of our garden wasps this usually means going underground – often in a hedge bank or similar well drained site. The queens can be seen drifting over such places in the spring, investigating every little cranny to see if it leads to a suitable spot. Many fail to find a home, but those that do quickly begin work. They often select existing cavities such as old mouse holes, but are well able to excavate new holes if necessary, bringing out the soil particles in their jaws. Then the building materials must be brought in.

Wasps build their nests with paper, which they produce by scraping wood from fences and other wooden structures with their jaws and mixing it with saliva to make a pulp – which they then form into flimsy sheets. It is common to see, and hear, the queen wasps scraping in the spring, especially when they are working on old hogweed stems and similar hollow stalks which amplify the sounds of their jaws. The queen builds a few six-sided cells in her chamber and lays an egg in each, and as soon as the eggs hatch she is fully occupied in feeding the grubs. The latter quickly develop into workers, and as soon as they emerge they take over the chores, leaving their mother to concentrate on egg-laying. They enlarge the nest cavity, when necessary, and add several more tiers of cells to the nest, which may be as large as a football by mid-summer. Up to 25,000 wasps may be produced in a single nest during the summer, although not all are alive at the same time. So why don't we see many wasps in the early part of the summer? They're too busy feeding their younger sisters – and a few young brothers. And here we can appreciate their great value to the gardener: while the adult wasps have a weakness for fruit and other sweet things, the grubs are reared almost entirely on meat – usually in the form of caterpillars and other insects. The occupants of a single nest may consume more than 250,000 insects during the summer, and, as many of these would otherwise have fed on our crops, the wasps are clearly doing us a service.

In their search for insects the worker wasps have to spread out over a wide area, and therefore remain rather inconspicuous, although several might gather to dismantle a dead bird or any piece of meat that you care to hang out for them. At the end of the summer, however, their work comes to an end. Males and new queens have already flown, and the old queen has stopped laying. There are no more grubs to rear and the workers retire to one long round of garden parties and orgies in the orchard, where ripe fruit is quickly reduced to empty skins. For a short time the wasps can certainly become a nuisance, but it *is* only a short time: most of the insects burn

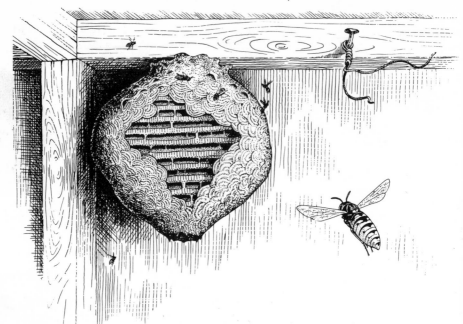

The nest of the common wasp built in the corner of a shed. The shell-like lobes of the outer covering are clearly seen, and the horizontal combs can also be seen where the covering has been cut away.

themselves out within a few weeks, and the rest succumb to the first frosts of the autumn.

Two species account for most of our garden wasps, although you'll have to get pretty close to them to distinguish them. They are the common wasp (*Vespula vulgaris*) and the German wasp (*V. germanica*). The former usually has an anchor-like mark on its face and narrow stripes on its thorax, while the German wasp has three black spots on its face and broader, bulging thoracic stripes. Both prefer to nest in the ground, although they will also use roof cavities and often hang their nests inside garden sheds: a secluded and protected site is the main requirement. A third species sometimes nests in the garden, and virtually replaces the other two in northern regions. This is the Norwegian wasp (*Dolichovespula norvegica*), distinguished from the others by a broad facial stripe and by having only two yellow spots at the rear of the thorax. It hangs its relatively small nest in bushes and clothes it with smooth, overlapping paper sheets. The nests of the common and German wasps are covered with delicate shell-like lobes of paper.

Face to face with the common wasp (left), *the German wasp* (centre) *and the Norwegian wasp.*

The striking yellow and black coats of the wasps, which give them their American name of yellow-jackets, are examples of warning coloration – advertising their stings and unpleasant flavours and warning birds and other predators to keep away. Of course, the predators have to learn the lesson first, and they usually do this when they are young and game for

The drone-fly (right) *is an excellent mimic of the honey bee.*

anything. They try a few wasps, find them unpleasant, and soon learn to associate the yellow and black pattern with the unpleasantness. Thereafter they avoid insects with this pattern. Many harmless and tasty insects cash in on this arrangement by sharing the wasps' colours. Hover-flies (see p. 80) are among the best exponents of this kind of mimicry, with several species resembling our social wasps. Many also mimic the solitary wasps. The resemblance is not necessarily very strong: all that is needed is a slight hesitation by the bird and the insect can escape. It works even with us: we have all drawn back at some time from a harmless hover-fly or wasp beetle in the belief that it was a wasp. Some of the resemblances, however, are extraordinarily close – the result of thousands of generations of natural selection during which predators continually remove the least efficient mimics. The best mimics are left to breed in each generation, and the resemblance between model and mimic gets better and better.

Solitary wasps

In terms of species, the social wasps are far outnumbered by the solitary ones, whose life stories are very similar to those of the solitary bees (see p. 99). Many share the black and yellow patterns of the social species, although others are completely black. As far as their breeding is concerned, the main difference between the solitary bees and the solitary wasps is that the latter all feed their grubs with insects or spiders instead of pollen and nectar. In this, of course, they resemble the social wasps but, whereas the latter chew up their victims and feed them to the growing larvae on demand,

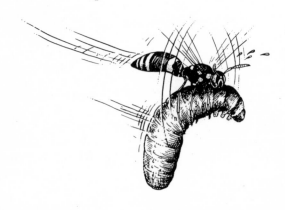

the solitary wasps generally stockpile their nests with whole prey which has been paralysed by the sting. Because it is not dead, the prey remains in good condition for however long the wasp grubs need it – often for several months.

Each kind of wasp has its preferred prey, with flies, aphids and caterpillars being the most frequently taken insects. Many of these are a nuisance in the garden, so the wasps should be welcomed and even encouraged to breed. They nest in similar situations to the solitary bees and can be attracted by the same kinds of artificial homes (see p. 99). The only trouble with this is that you might spend rather a lot of time watching the antics of the wasps as they try to squeeze plump caterpillars into holes that seem too small. But they go in eventually: the wasps are properly programmed and don't waste time on prey that won't go into their nest holes.

Some odd nest sites

Most of our solitary bees and wasps excavate nest chambers in the ground or in dead wood, but they are not slow to take advantage of existing cavities and thus avoid a lot of hard work. Several kinds of mason bee (Osmia spp) make use of empty snail shells in which to construct their little earthenware cells, and there is a well documented case of one of these bees using an old door lock as a nursery. The key-hole provided easy access and the bee managed to fit 53 small cells into the lock cavity. Some years ago I noticed a mason wasp taking a great deal of interest in my porch, but it wasn't until I went to open a small sliding window that I discovered what the wasp had been up to. It had constructed several cells in the groove of the window track and neatly plastered over them so that I could not slide the window back. On another occasion I discovered a mason wasp building in

the narrow cavity along the spine of an old book. The latter lived on a window sill and I can imagine the wasp making mad dashes to collect fresh building materials every time the window was opened. I've no idea if it ever managed to complete the job.

Bumble bees sometimes nest in unusual situations, although when you realize that some of them frequently set up home in old birds' nests the artificial sites don't seem so odd. Bird boxes are commonly used, giving good protection from the weather and from marauding mice, but not from the hornet: I have watched a queen hornet systematically remove bumble bee grubs from a nest box over a period of days and cart them off to feed her own grubs. One queen bumble bee I met set up home in a bicycle saddle bag in the shed – a site commonly used by birds as well.

The handsome hornet

The hornet is Europe's largest social wasp and easily recognized by its large size and its brown and yellow coat. It is widely distributed and common on the Continent, but has always been on the edge of its range in Britain and its numbers fluctuate a great deal. It was quite common in the southern counties in the first half of this century, but the population crashed in the 1950s and for a couple of decades the hornet was rarely seen outside the New Forest and parts of East Anglia. More efficient forestry methods were suggested as one cause for the decline, for the insect always seemed to nest in hollow trees and these are just the trees that are removed when forests are 'improved'. Climatic changes might also have been involved in the hornet's decline. In recent years, however – since the 1976 heatwave, it seems – the insect has been spreading again. There has been a dramatic increase in the eastern counties and the Midlands and the hornet is regularly seen foraging in gardens. There is no obvious explanation for this increase, but it may be that the insects have learnt to use a wider variety of nest sites. Nests have been found in sheds and garages, and I have seen several built in the cavities of old walls. This would certainly explain the spread of what was once very much a woodland insect into the garden habitat. Despite their size, hornets are not aggressive insects and rarely sting people. They eat a lot of other insects including smaller wasps, butterflies and bumble bees (see p. 109).

Swarms of ants

Two main kinds of ant live in our gardens – the red ants that sting and the black ants that don't. If you have rough, grassy areas – in an orchard for example – you may have yellow ants as well. The red and black ants often nest under stones and paths, and the red ants may also occupy old logs and tree stumps. The yellow ant usually builds conspicuous mounds of soil. Each nest contains one or more egg-laying queens and a number of workers, the latter all being sterile females. As with bees and wasps, the workers do all the chores and they spend much of their time foraging. They collect seeds and honeydew (see p. 54) and also gather lots of small insects. Many of the latter are garden pests, and so the ants are quite useful to have around. The only time they really cause any damage is when they nest under plants and nibble the roots or instal aphids on them, thus causing the plants to wilt and sometimes to die. You can sometimes see ants marching to and from a particularly good food source, the columns being most obvious when the

A section through a black ant nest and (inset) *workers moving pupal cocoons after disturbance of the nest.*

trails go up and down tree trunks or along fence rails. The black ant occasionally invades houses if it finds a supply of sweet food, but otherwise ants remain pretty inconspicuous until the 'wedding day'.

During the summer, when temperatures are high and plenty of food is available, the colony begins to rear males and new queens, which, unlike the workers, have wings. But they do not leave the nest right away. The workers keep them indoors until conditions are right for the 'wedding flight'. This generally takes place on a sunny afternoon and, with our garden ants, most often occurs in August. Triggered off by the weather, all the nests in an area open at the same time and the familiar plagues of flying ants begin. Males from neighbouring colonies join together to form huge dancing swarms, to which the females are attracted and then grabbed by partners. Mating takes place in the air or on the ground, depending on the species, and the males die soon afterwards, but the mated queens, each endowed with enough sperm to last a lifetime of several years, are about to start work. Of course, very

A young female, possibly a future queen, takes to the air for her one and only flight.

few ever reach this stage, for the mating swarm is a nutritious target for all the swallows and martins in the area and many of the ants are snapped up within minutes of leaving their nests.

The first chore for the newly mated queen is to break off her wings, for she will not fly again. She may enter an existing nest of her own species, but she is more likely to hide away under a stone and begin a new colony in the spring. Like the bees and wasps, she has to rear a small brood of workers herself, but as soon as these first workers are mature they take over the job of building and running the nest, leaving their mother to concentrate on egg-laying.

Ichneumons – the insidious invaders

Leggy, chestnut-brown insects like the one pictured opposite often enter lighted windows on summer evenings, and then buzz frantically up and down the glass as they try to get out again. They are ichneumons, often known as ichneumon flies, although they are not true flies. They belong to the same major group of insects as bees and wasps. There are thousands of species, with slender bodies anything up to about 4 cm (1³/5 inches) long and rather shiny wings which are laid flat over the body at rest. Most species are brown or black, sometimes with yellow markings, but such is the range of size and general appearance that it is not always easy to say 'ichneumon' right away. If you have a lens, try counting the antennal segments: if there are sixteen or more you can be pretty sure you have an ichneumon. Or you can use a process of elimination: if it's got a 'wasp waist' and doesn't look like a bee or an ant or a wasp, it's quite probably an ichneumon.

All ichneumons are parasites in their young stages, their main hosts being

The grubs of Apanteles glomeratus, *a common parasite of the large white caterpillar, emerging from the dead and shrivelled body of the host.*

the caterpillars of butterflies and moths. The females scuttle over vegetation with their antennae quivering excitedly as they search for the scents of their victims. Having found a suitable caterpillar, the ichneumon stabs it with her ovipositor and lays one or more eggs in it.* The ichneumon grubs then develop inside the host, carefully avoiding the vital organs at first and finally killing it when they are fully grown. The grubs then pupate inside or outside the shrivelled caterpillar skin. Parasitized caterpillars are rather lethargic and frequently sit forlornly on the upper surfaces of leaves while their healthier siblings tuck themselves safely away: not surprising, therefore, that the average caterpillar collector finds a rather high proportion of parasitized individuals in his cages (see p. 76). The ichneumon's ovipositor is usually quite short and often hardly visible, but some of the larger species,

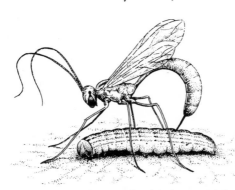

* A few ichneumons lay their eggs on the outside of the hosts and their grubs feed externally.

including the *Ophion*, pictured on the previous page, can deliver a small prick, accompanied by a slight stinging sensation, if handled. Some species, not normally found in the garden, have ovipositors as long as or longer than their bodies. These usually seek out victims that are concealed in galls or other plant tissues, relying on minute vibrations as well as scent to locate their hidden hosts.

A few ichneumons are hyperparasites, attacking insects which are themselves already living as parasites inside other species. This necessitates a refined location mechanism and is an excellent variation of Swift's observation:

> So, naturalists, observe a flea
> Hath smaller fleas that on him prey;
> And these have smaller fleas to bite 'em,
> And so proceed *ad infinitum*.

There are, indeed, parasites of hyperparasites, but we now are getting into the realms of some extremely tiny insects.

EIGHT LEGS:
THE SPIDERS AND THEIR KIN

Do you like spiders? The chances are that you don't. You might well be one of the thousands of people with a real fear of these animals, for 'arachnophobia' – a posh name for a fear of spiders – is one of the commonest of all phobias. But at the same time, you probably obey the old rhyme:

> If you wish to live and thrive
> Let a spider run alive.

These two conflicting attitudes towards spiders can be found in human societies throughout the world. The idea that it is unlucky to kill a spider may stem from the usefulness of the animals, for we all know that spiders kill and eat large numbers of troublesome flies, but it is less easy to see why they should be feared so much. Some are potentially dangerous to human life, admittedly, but these are very few and you won't find them wandering around the British countryside. The house spider that ambles over your

floor is perfectly harmless, and yet it sends people jumping onto tables. When I tried to discover the reason for this odd behaviour, the long, hairy legs were mentioned by several people. Pointing out that these same people had no fear of Afghan hounds, I was gently reminded that dogs have only four legs – spiders·have eight! Could this be a clue? Most people have a fear of octopuses as well!

Whatever your feelings towards spiders, the animals exist in vast numbers in your garden and many enter your house. You can't avoid them, so you might as well learn to live with them. Discover something of their fascinating lives and habits and you'll find yourself developing a sneaking admiration for the animals. At the same time your fear could well subside. The spiders and their relatives, which include the scorpions and harvestmen and assorted other beasties, belong with the insects in the enormous group known as arthropods, which we met on page 41. But jointed legs are among the few features that insects and spiders have in common. As we have already seen, spiders have eight legs instead of the six found in insects. They never have wings and they don't have antennae, although a pair of slender palps at the front may look and act like antennae. All these 8-legged arthropods belong to the class known as arachnids.

The spider's hairy body

A spider's body is clearly divided into two parts by a narrow waist and both parts are commonly rather hairy. The hairs are often brightly coloured, although some spider colours are due to pigments in the body wall. The front part of the body, known as the cephalothorax (literally the 'head-chest'), carries the four pairs of legs and, in front of them, the palps. The latter spring from around the mouth and are well supplied with sensitive hairs and other sense organs. They help the spider to smell, taste and feel its way about. The bristly legs are also very sensitive and, together with the bristles on the general body surface, they can detect the scents of nearby animals as well as the minute air currents caused by their movements. The palps of female spiders look very much like short legs, but the male palps are generally strongly clubbed and, as we shall see, they play a major role in courtship and mating.

In front of the palps and partly hidden under the front of the body are the fangs, which in almost all spiders are connected to poison glands. The spiders are all predatory creatures and they use their poison to paralyse or kill their prey. Very few are able to harm us: most are unable to pierce our skin, and those that can get through don't usually have enough venom to produce more than minor irritation. There is no reason to fear the bite of any British spider. The animals won't even attempt to bite unless roughly handled, for human skin doesn't tickle a spider's palate. Insects are the spiders' main victims, but many other spiders are eaten as well and cannibalism is quite common. Many fascinating techniques are used for capturing prey, and admiration for their skill and cunning plays a major role in spider folklore.

Spiders have no real jaws to chew their food and they can take in only liquid nourishment. Most have sharp teeth at the base of each fang and these are used to shred and grind the prey. The basal parts of the palps can also be brought together to crush the food. Digestive juices poured out from the mouth gradually convert the crushed material into soup, which the spider can suck up. Just a bundle of indigestible rubbish remains.

Most of our spiders have eight eyes, arranged in various patterns on the front and top of the cephalothorax. The arrangement of the eyes is of great help in identifying the various spider families. But even with eight eyes, many of our spiders don't see too well: scent and touch are far more important than sight to most of them, although we shall meet a few sharp-sighted hunters as we explore the garden. A few spiders have only six eyes, but, whether there are six or eight, each eye has only a single lens and there are no compound eyes such as we have seen in the insects.

The rear section of the body is the abdomen, which may be slim or distinctly podgy – just like people really. The breathing and reproductive organs open on the underside of the abdomen, but the most obvious features of this region are the all-important spinners, through which the spider's silk emerges. All spiders produce silk, although they don't all use it to make webs.

The spider's silk

Silk is produced in a number of glands in the spider's abdomen and emerges through the three pairs of spinners at or just under the tip of the body. The spinners are quite large and clearly visible in some species, including the house spiders, but in many others they are small and concealed from above. The silk cannot be squeezed out like toothpaste from a tube and must be drawn from the spinners – usually by the legs. It is liquid to start with, but solidifies into threads as soon as it is stretched.

At least five different kinds of silk gland are known to be connected to the spinners, each gland producing a different kind of silk. One kind of silk is used to form the drag-lines and life-lines that spiders trail behind them wherever they go and on which they lower themselves gently to the ground when disturbed. This same type of silk is used for most web-building, although it does not form the spiral threads of the familiar wheel-shaped orb webs (see p. 120). A second kind of silk is used only for the attachment pads which join the drag-lines to the ground or other surfaces. A third kind is used for wrapping prey and also for the outer wall of the egg sac (see p. 138). A fourth kind, produced only by females, forms the inner lining of the egg sac. These four types of silk are produced by all spiders, but the fifth is found only in the orb-web spiders (see p. 120), which use it to make the spiral parts of their webs. A sixth type of gland, not strictly a silk gland, produces the gum that coats the spiral threads.

Each gland leads to its own minute pores on the appropriate spinner, so the spider doesn't have to bother about connecting up the right glands. It merely has to remember which kind of silk to produce for the job in hand – but this is instinctively controlled and the spider can actually produce two or three different kinds of silk at one time.

Next time you walk into a spider's web stretched across the garden path or decorating the shed door, try to appreciate the strength and elasticity of the silk. Although a good deal finer than silkworm silk, it is surprisingly tough and does not break immediately. In fact, spider silk is stronger than steel wire of the same thickness. So why don't we use spider silk for fabrics? It has been done: a very patient Frenchman named Bon produced a few pairs of spider silk gloves and stockings early in the 18th century, but the silk is so fine – no more than 0.004 mm in diameter in the webs of our garden spider – that it does not stand up at all well to machine spinning and weaving. At about the time of M. Bon's gloves, the prominent French scientist Réné Réaumur was asked to investigate the feasibility of using spider silk on a large scale. He estimated that 663,552 spiders would have to be collected to yield a single pound of silk. Fewer spiders would be needed if they could be reared and 'milked' regularly, but each would have to be kept in a separate cage and regularly fed with flies. End of story. By comparison, today's well bred silkworms, slightly more productive than those of Réaumur's day, give a pound of silk from just 2,000 individuals – and they're much easier to rear than spiders. The only real uses for spider silk are those devised by the spiders themselves, although the finest threads are sometimes used in optical equipment to divide up the field of view. If you cut yourself you can try the old-fashioned treatment of a few cobweb layers placed over the cut to stop the bleeding. The fine mesh of the household cobweb readily traps the blood corpuscles and promotes scab formation.

Catching food – the web-spinners

The spider's web is among the very few traps constructed by animals. The only other British examples are the nets spun by certain caddis fly larvae. These are spun in running water and they snare assorted plant and animal food drifting down with the current. Looking at an exquisitely constructed orb web, it is not easy to appreciate how such a complex structure could have come into being. But it's all a matter of evolution. Webs must have originated from the tangled drag-lines that surrounded the early spiders' lairs and egg cocoons. Insects would have become trapped here and the untidiest spiders probably did quite well for food. They didn't have to go hunting as much as their tidier relatives and, having more time and energy to breed, they produced plenty of untidy offspring to carry on the trend. Many refinements were necessary before the orb web appeared, but there was plenty of time for today's wide range of web designs to come into existence.

The garden spider.

The more or less circular orb webs, spun by the garden spider (*Araneus diadematus*) and its relatives in the family Argiopidae, are the most conspicuous and familiar webs in the garden, especially in the late summer and autumn when they are at their largest and often made even more obvious by dew or frost. They are masterpieces of silken engineering, and yet the spiders never have a geometry lesson in their lives – or any other lesson for that matter: few spiders ever have any contact with their mothers and their activities are entirely instinctive. When you've an hour or so to spare, try a bit of spider watching. You'll learn more about webs and their construction in this way than you will from any book. Early morning is a good time to find the spiders at work on their webs, for insects blundering into the webs during the night often do a lot of damage and the spiders often have to re-build after a good feast. But late risers needn't miss the fun: I've watched garden spiders building and re-building their webs at all hours of day and night. The work is done when necessary, and if you can't actually find one at work you can be a real rotter and *make* it perform. Gently cut the circular part away from the framework of the web and then settle down and watch – and watch and watch, if you follow the advice of T.H. Savory in his fascinating book *The Spider's Web*. The spider will often re-build in the existing frame and, unlike some builders I have met, it gets on with the job without delay. But the spider has a big incentive: it gets no dinner until the job is done.

An alternative method of getting an orb-web spider to work for you is to remove the spider from its web and place it on a loop of stout wire between 30 and 50 cm (12 to 20 inches) in diameter. Hang the loop from a convenient support and, with luck, the spider will make a nice web inside the wire. But be prepared to retrieve the animal on several occasions if it gets fed up with the experiment and wanders off.

I can do no more here than give a brief outline of the main stages in the building of an orb web. You'll be able to fill in the details from your own observations. The first requirement is the establishment of the bridge thread, which forms the upper edge of the frame. It can be established in one of two ways. Generally, the spider anchors a drag-line at a convenient spot and then walks around, trailing the line, until she finds another suitable anchorage. The line is then hauled tight and fixed firmly in place. Alternatively, the spider may draw a strand of silk from her spinners and let it blow in the wind. The pull of the wind drags more and more silk out until it catches on some support. Using her remarkable ability to assess the tension and strength of the line, the spider decides whether or not it is safe to cross. If all seems well, she makes the crossing and anchors the far end securely

STAGES IN BUILDING AN ORB WEB

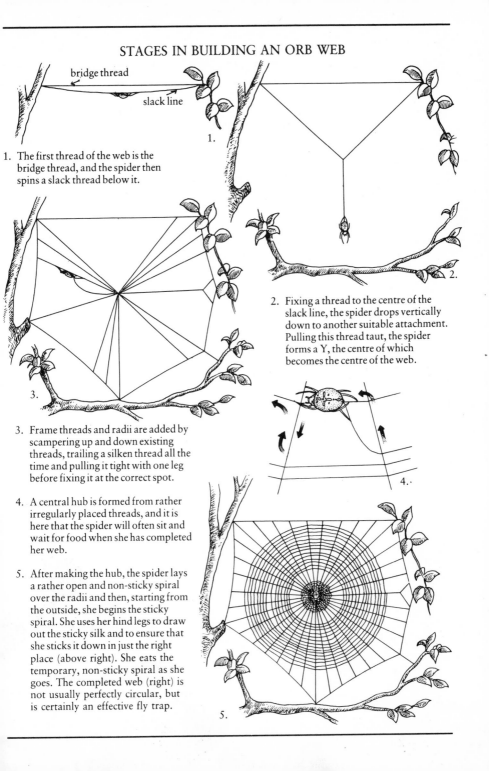

1. The first thread of the web is the bridge thread, and the spider then spins a slack thread below it.

2. Fixing a thread to the centre of the slack line, the spider drops vertically down to another suitable attachment. Pulling this thread taut, the spider forms a Y, the centre of which becomes the centre of the web.

3. Frame threads and radii are added by scampering up and down existing threads, trailing a silken thread all the time and pulling it tight with one leg before fixing it at the correct spot.

4. A central hub is formed from rather irregularly placed threads, and it is here that the spider will often sit and wait for food when she has completed her web.

5. After making the hub, the spider lays a rather open and non-sticky spiral over the radii and then, starting from the outside, she begins the sticky spiral. She uses her hind legs to draw out the sticky silk and to ensure that she sticks it down in just the right place (above right). She eats the temporary, non-sticky spiral as she goes. The completed web (right) is not usually perfectly circular, but is certainly an effective fly trap.

before strengthening the bridge with more strands of silk. Details vary from now on, but the spider commonly spins a slack thread which hangs from the bridge like a washing line. She then drops vertically from the centre of this line and anchors the new vertical thread to a branch or to the ground. She pulls it tight and pulls the 'washing line' into a V. The point of the V becomes the centre of the web and at this stage, as you can see from the drawings, the three primary spokes or radii have been established. The difficult part is now over, and by scampering up and down the radii with trailing threads the spider quickly forms the rest of the frame and inserts the additional spokes. Notice how deftly the legs are used to guide and position the threads.

When all the spokes are in place, the spider lays a rather open spiral over them, starting near the centre. This is only a temporary feature and, like the spokes, it has no gum. Then comes the final stage – the placing of the sticky spiral. This work begins at the outside and, although the sticky thread is more or less continuous, one glance will show that it does not form a perfect spiral. The hub is usually above the centre and the lower part of the web has many overlapping arcs, laid down as the spider moves to and fro across this area as if she were on a pendulum. She uses her legs as rulers, and the speed and accuracy with which the thread is attached to the spokes are truly amazing. The temporary spiral, which was no more than scaffolding, is eaten as the spider works her way to the centre with the sticky spiral. Thrifty animal that she is, she also eats the old silk when she dismantles her web prior to re-building.

The sticky spiral is coated with gum as it is spun, but the gum breaks into droplets as the thread is stretched and it is these droplets that glisten with dew in the morning. If you watch closely you will see that the spider walks only on the non-sticky spokes and does not tangle with the gum, but she has oily secretions on her feet that prevent her from sticking to it in any case. In addition, the web is usually slightly off vertical and the spider keeps to the lower surface so that her body hangs away from the web and does not touch the threads. The sticky spiral does not extend right to the centre of the web, where many spiders build a silken platform on which to rest. Between this platform and the sticky spiral there is a free zone, through which the spider can get to the other side of the web when necessary.

The whole web-building process generally takes less than an hour and is repeated every day or two, even if the web is undamaged. The gum is the problem: it does not actually dry, but becomes coated with dust and therefore becomes less sticky and less effective.

Ingenious experimenters have shown, by covering the spiders' eyes, that the animals don't need to see what they are doing: everything is done by touch, and so they have no problems with web-making at night. Spiders taken into space on one of the American Skylab missions also showed us that they don't need gravity to help them: they built perfect webs despite complete weightlessness.

I have followed convention and referred to the spider as 'she' in the above description of web-building, but this doesn't mean that males don't spin webs – how else could they eat? There is, however, a reason behind the convention: adult males, which are in any case smaller and less conspicuous than the females, tend to abandon food in favour of sex, and so most of the large spiders that we see spinning webs *are* females.

Not a bad hour's work

The completed garden spider's web clearly shows the irregular maze of threads forming the central platform, with a noticeable gap between this and the sticky spiral. It is commonly markedly asymmetrical, with the hub much nearer the top than the bottom. If you've ever wondered how much silk goes into a web, why not try measuring it? The easiest way is to bring a lightly gummed dark card up behind the web and collect the whole thing for measurement at your leisure. A large web I examined recently had 31 spokes averaging about 20 cm (8 inches) in length, and in the lower half of the web there were 22 arcs of the sticky spiral. Including the frame, I estimated that the web contained nearly 30 metres of silk. But so fine is the silk – 0.003 mm is a typical diameter for garden spider silk – that even a large web weighs well under 0.5 mg. The fact that it can support a spider 4,000 times its own weight – and also snare prey weighing a good deal more than this – testifies to the excellent design of the web with its thousand or so junctions. Not a bad hour's work indeed.

But if you want to see some really big webs, take a trip to south-east Asia, where species of *Nephila* make webs up to 2 metres across. Hold on to your hat on forest paths if you don't want it knocked off by one of these webs or its guy lines. Birds are commonly caught in these webs, and the silk is so strong that local people use the webs to make fishing nets.

WHO'S WHO AMONG THE SPIDERS

Just over 600 different kinds of spider live in the British Isles and a good many of them can turn up in the garden. Fifty of them are orb-web spiders, spinning their familiar wheel-shaped webs on fences and other man-made structures as well as on the vegetation. The following are just four of the commonest garden species:

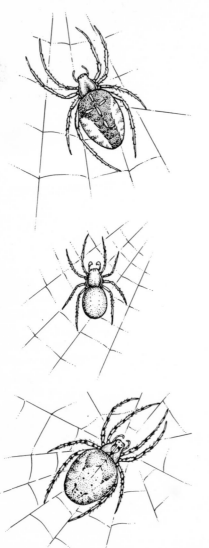

ARANEUS DIADEMATUS, the garden spider, ranges from fawn, through orange, to a very dark brown, but can always be recognized by the white cross-like pattern on the abdomen. It is sometimes called the cross spider. The female's body is about 12mm (½ inch) long when she is mature in late summer. Look for her web on trees, shrubs and fences. It may reach 40 cm (15 inches) in diameter. The spider usually rests in a nearby shelter during the day, but you can see her in the centre of the web from dusk onwards.

ARANIELLA CUCURBITINA has a beautiful pale green abdomen and a shiny brown front half. There is a bright red patch just under the tip of the abdomen. Only 6 mm (¼ inch) long, the spider spins a small web in trees and bushes, usually at least 1.5 m (¼ feet) above the ground, often at just the right height for you to see it in the hedge. The web may be spun on a single leaf, whose edges are drawn in slightly to form a shallow dish. The spider is mature from late spring onwards.

META SEGMENTATA is perhaps the commonest of our garden-dwelling orb-web spiders. Its colour varies a lot, but there are usually two dark triangular patches at the front of the abdomen and the cephalothorax carries a dark mark like a miniature tuning fork – although you will need a lens to see it. The web is slung fairly low down in the hedge or in herbaceous vegetation, generally at a marked angle to the vertical, and it has no central platform, although the spider often sits there. Look for it from spring to late summer. Unlike most spiders, the male is almost as large as his mate – 6 mm (¼ inch) long to her 8 mm (⅓ inch) – and he can often be seen sitting at the edge of her web in the summer.

ZYGIELLA X-NOTATA generally spins her web on walls and fences and very often chooses the corner of a doorway or a window frame. The web is easily recognized because the sticky spiral is missing from two sectors near the top. The spoke running through this empty space serves as the signal thread, and by following it you can find the spider's retreat – generally tucked away in a crevice. The spider's abdomen bears a fairly distinct, greyish leaf-like pattern, often surrounded by a pinkish tinge, but you won't normally see her until after dark. She is 6–7 mm (about ¼ inch) long and the only one of our orb-web spiders that remains active throughout the year; the others pass the winter in the egg stage or as dormant individuals.

Feeding time

Most of our orb-weavers spend the daytime in a shelter near the web, but always in contact with it by a silken thread. They have no set meal times and rush out whenever an insect blunders into the web and sends vibrations along the signal line. It is possible to lure several kinds of spiders from their retreats by touching their webs with a vibrating tuning fork. E above middle

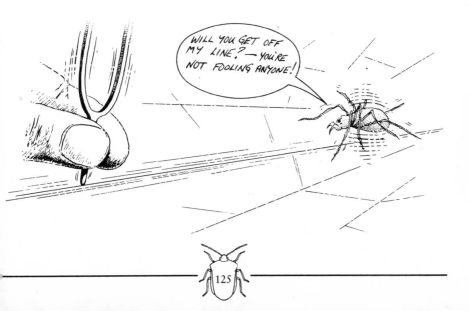

C is said to be the best frequency, but this has nothing to do with the spiders musical tastes – it merely approximates to the vibrations set up by a struggling fly. Dashing to the centre of the web, the spider soon works out where the vibrations are coming from and glides along the appropriate spoke. Her subsequent behaviour depends largely on the size of the visitor and the intensity of its struggles. Small victims are bitten immediately, but larger ones are generally wrapped in silk before they are bitten. The spider deftly draws wide bands of silk from her spinners with her hind legs, while her front legs spin the victim's body like a spool until it is completely shrouded like a mummy. The fatal bite is delivered and the spider then carts the bundle to the hub of the web or to her retreat to enjoy her meal. If she is not hungry she may leave the trussed corpse in the web for a while, but she risks losing her prize if she leaves it for too long: there are thieves about in the world of creepy-crawlies just as in human society. Wasps of various kinds are happy to plunder flies and other loot from the spider's web, and even the flimsy scorpion fly (see p. 46) is willing to risk its life for an easy meal, but the greatest rogues in this respect are other spiders.

The value of spiders in our battle with insect pests was vividly brought home to me one day when I noticed that all the webs on my trees and shrubs were studded with aphids. I counted 409 aphids in one garden spider web measuring a mere 14 cm (5½ inches) across, and saw similar densities in dozens of other webs. The aphids were not being eaten, but they *were* being caught and the spiders were doing my garden plants a great favour. The late W.S. Bristowe, one of our greatest spider watchers, once estimated that the weight of insects caught and eaten by spiders each year in Britain exceeds the weight of the human population.

Spiders will eat almost any kind of insect, although each species has its preferred size range and won't tackle anything too big. Bumble bees, for example, are quickly released by our orb-web spiders, although their powerful struggles often set them free without help from the web's proprietor. There is also a minimum size below which it just isn't worth bothering about, but clearly small spiders will accept smaller prey than larger ones. Wasps are fair game for most adult orb-web spiders, which are not impressed by the warning coloration even if they can see it. There are, however, some boldly marked insects that the spiders will not accept. Try throwing a magpie moth (see p. 76) into a web if you really want to upset a spider. One taste of the moth is enough to send the spider into a frenzy, rapidly cutting the insect from the web and then rushing off to clean palps and fangs. Fluid is often poured from the mouth at this point, almost as if

he spider is being sick after its unpleasant encounter. Many bugs and
awflies are also unpalatable to spiders, and so are the harvestmen that
commonly blunder into webs.

Lace on the wall

Take a look at almost any old brick wall and you'll see several more or less
circular webs looking like scruffy lace doilies. Each surrounds a hole, in
which lurks the web's creator – a spider called *Amaurobius*. On a dry wall it
is likely to be *A. similis*, up to 12 mm ($\frac{1}{2}$ inch) long and with a pale brown
abdomen marked with black as shown in the illustration. You will also find
this spider on shed walls and close-boarded fences. On damper walls the
webs are more likely to belong to the very similar, but slightly smaller *A.
fenestralis*. You can find these webs throughout the year. Unlike those of
the orb-web spiders, they are not re-made each day; the spider merely adds

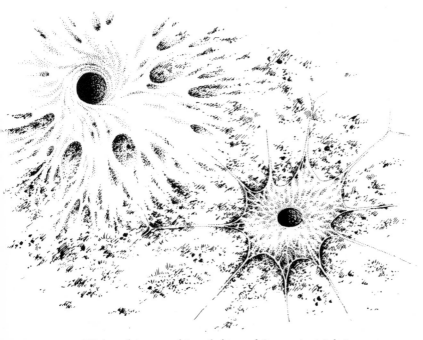

Webs of Amaurobius (left) *and* Segestria (right).

127

a few more strands of silk as necessary, and this gives the webs their scruffy look. Spinning takes place soon after nightfall, and here you needn't curse those run-down batteries because *Amaurobius* dislikes the light and will stop work if your torch is too bright. She spins four threads simultaneously. Two remain straight, like miniature tram-lines, but the other two pass over the vibrating legs and are thrown into loops before being laid over the 'tram-lines'. At the same time, *Amaurobius* produces her speciality – hundreds of extremely fine threads drawn out from a perforated plate just in front of the spinners. These threads, which are bluish when fresh, are laid over the other strands in a dense band. They are not gummy, but trap the feet of any insect crawling over them as surely as any glue and also cling tightly to any roughness on your fingers – the same way that nylon stockings catch on any roughness of the skin. Prey is almost always bitten on the leg by *Amaurobius* and then dragged into the retreat. Try charming the spider out with a tuning fork: it usually responds even more readily than the orb-web spiders.

While looking at *Amaurobius* webs, keep your eyes open for the cunning snare of *Segestria senoculata*, a brownish sausage of a spider up to 10 mm (²/₅ inch) long. One of the 6-eyed species, it takes up residence in a deep crevice and spins a small circular collar around the entrance. But this is not the real trap: look carefully around the collar and you will see a dozen or so trip-wires radiating from it. The spider sits in her retreat with her toes on the collar, and as soon as anything stumbles over one of the threads she is out to investigate in a flash.

Shimmering hammocks

The most dramatic demonstration of our immense spider population comes in the autumn, when webs sparkle with dew or frost and show up much more clearly. Every branch of shrub and hedgerow seems to bear a silvery hammock, supported by a maze of scaffolding above and below. These webs belong to the large group known as linyphiids, which account for about 250 of the 620 known kinds of British spiders. By far the commonest in the garden is *Linyphia triangularis*, up to 6 mm (¼ inch) long with a distinctly triangular abdomen and a row of dark triangular marks down the middle. Look for the spider hanging upside down under the web. The latter is normally slightly domed, but sags in the familiar hammock shape when weighed down with dew. Plant hoppers and other small insects bump into the scaffolding and fall on to the sheet, getting their feet thoroughly tangled n the mesh before the spider scampers along to bite them and drag them down through the sheet. If the insects manage to cling to the scaffolding the spider will actually shake the web until they fall.

The small silken sheets that adorn the lawn belong to the numerous relatives of *Linyphia* known as money spiders. In rough grass there is scarcely a blade untouched by one of these webs. There is little scaffolding above them and the small dark spiders exist on springtails and other tiny jumpers that land on the sheets.

Slaughter on the scaffold

Imagine yourself blown off your feet in a howling gale and flung towards a scaffolded building. The chances of passing straight through the scaffolding are slim, and if some of the poles were coated with super-glue you would be held fast. This is exactly what happens to small insects flying into the scaffold webs of the theridiid spiders. This group, characterized by a distinctly globular abdomen, contains the infamous American black widow spider, said to enjoy lurking under the seats of outside loos — probably not a bad place to catch small flies. Most species sling their flimsy 3-dimensional webs in the vegetation, with the central part of the maze studded with blobs of gum. When insects arrive, the spider gingerly throws more silk over them to immobilize them before moving in for the fatal bite. Quite large insects can be over-powered in this way. Familiar theridiids of our British gardens include Theridion sisyphium, *whose family life is revealed on p. 140, and* Enoplognatha ovata. *The latter is most often discovered curled up in a leaf with its*

bluish green egg sac. About 4 mm
(¹/₆ inch) long, it has a cream
abdomen often decorated with a broad
carmine stripe down the centre or two
more slender stripes at the sides.

The family life of Sisyphium, *with mother feeding her babies below the thimble-like shelter* (see p. 140). *The irregular mesh of the scaffold web can be seen around the spiders.*

Hairy house spiders

Sheet webs are also built by the large house spiders that scuttle over our floors and often take up involuntary residence in the bath – having climbed or fallen in only to find the sides too slippery even for spiders' feet. These webs are the familiar cobwebs, slung in the corners of neglected rooms, sheds and other out-buildings. Unlike the sheets of the linyphiids, the

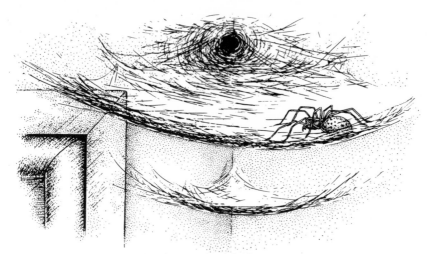

The sheet web of the house spider.

generally have a tubular retreat in the corner. Flies landing on the web quickly find their feet trapped in the maze of silk threads that form the sheet, and the spider has no trouble at all in carting them off to her parlour after a couple of paralysing bites. She doesn't bother to wrap her food – again unlike the linyphiids – and she can, as is often necessary in houses, go without food for weeks on end. There are several rather similar species, all endowed with the long legs which seem to upset so many people. How they manage to scamper over their webs without entangling their own legs is something that we have yet to discover.

Catching food – the ambushers

The ambushers are rather lazy spiders that don't bother with webs. They merely settle down in places likely to be frequented by insects and wait for their meals to arrive. The best known of these ambushers are the crab spiders of the family Thomisidae – rather squat and flat spiders with the first two pairs of legs longer and sturdier than the others. When disturbed, they scuttle sideways, just like a crab. Most crab spiders like to lurk in flowers and are often coloured to match their favourite blooms. Apart from concealing the spiders from their enemies, this camouflage also gives them the element of surprise against their prey, which sometimes lands right on top of them. Slow, deliberate movements bring the spider to face its victim, and then a sudden lunge sees the prey held down by the spider's front legs and the fangs sunk deep in the neck. The crab spiders always go for the neck, for an insect's nerves are concentrated here and a bite delivered just behind the head produces paralysis much more quickly than a bite given elsewhere.

Scent and vibration play a part in detecting prey, but sight is involved in the final lunge, and if you get your lens out and look a crab spider in the face you will see some much more prominent eyes than are found in the web-spinning spiders. Crab spiders are more active by day than by night.

The crab spiders have no teeth at the base of the fangs and cannot break up their prey. After injecting digestive juices, they simply suck up the resulting soup and leave the tough exoskeleton intact. Many entomologists

Dicing with death, a fly gets perilously near to a crab spider.

have been attracted to 'perfect' insects, only to find that crab spiders have got their first and left only empty shells clinging to the flowers.

The commonest crab spider on our garden flowers is *Misumena vatia*, although it occurs only in the southern half of the British Isles. Often known as the white death, the female is about 10 mm (²/₅ inch) long and generally white or pale yellow. She lurks in flowers of these colours and can actually change her own colour slowly if you move her from white to yellow flowers or vice-versa. The male is brownish and only about 4 mm (¹/₆ inch) long. The commonest of all our crab spiders is *Xysticus cristatus*, a brown creature about 7 mm (¼ inch) long and usually with prominent triangular marks on the abdomen. It is not attracted to flowers and can be found on the ground or on low vegetation, often in the hedge bottom, in spring and early summer. Unlike most spiders, it happily feeds on ants – as long as they are not too small. Crab spiders can't be bothered with anything less than about ¹/₆th of their own size, although they don't seem to mind how big their victims are. Butterflies and even bumble bees commonly fall victim to flower-haunting crab spiders.

Catching food – the hunters

The hunting spiders are not content to sit and wait for food to come to them: they go out and actively hunt for food. These hunters belong to several different groups and they include both diurnal and nocturnal prowlers. Touch, sight and chemical senses are all employed in varying degrees to find their prey.

When tidying up in the shed or moving logs or large stones in the garden you might well meet a mousy brown or slightly pinkish spider with prominent spinners. This is likely to be *Drassodes lapidosus*, up to 15 mm (³/₅ inch) long and one of our fiercest and bravest hunters. It spends the daytime in a silk-lined bedroom, under stones or in other secluded places, and gets up to hunt at night. It takes a wide range of prey, including many other spiders, which it finds mainly by smell and touch: the eyes are relatively small and inefficient. I'm not suggesting that you go in for spider-fighting, but when *Drassodes* is pitted against a spider larger than itself it puts on a great performance, beautifully described in Bristowe's

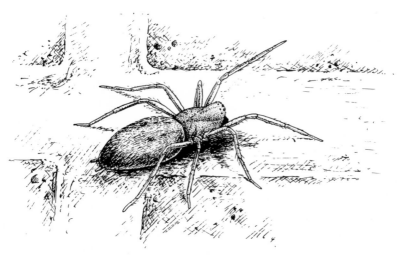

Drassodes lapidosus

fascinating book *The World of Spiders*. Cleverly avoiding the threatening fangs, *Drassodes* deftly darts around her opponent and anchors it to the ground with a wide band of silk before leaping on its back and plunging in her own fangs. The 'fight' may be over in less than a second.

Herpyllus blackwalli, a close relative of *Drassodes*, could be the 'something nasty in the woodshed', for this rather greasy-looking spider has been reported to bite people without provocation – although the bite is in no way dangerous. Up to 11 mm (½ inch) long, with black and grey hair, it is perhaps even more mouse-like than *Drassodes*. It is not uncommon in the house as well as in out-buildings, and it scours the walls and ceilings for prey at night. It is less bold than its cousin, however, and faced with a large adversary it is more likely to run away and use its silken ribbon as a protective fence.

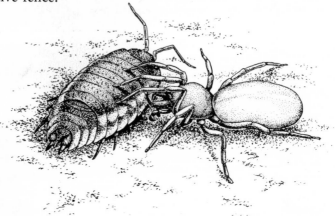

Dysdera *manages to get its huge jaws into a woodlouse.*

Turning over logs and stones or lifting clumps of aubretia and other low-growing plants, especially those draped over old walls, may bring you face to face with *Dysdera*, one of our most striking nocturnal hunters. The chestnut carapace and smooth, flesh-coloured abdomen readily identify this 6-eyed spider, but the most obvious features are the huge fangs. These are used for slaying woodlice, which few other spiders will touch – partly because of the repellent fluids but also because few spiders have the necessary armour-piercing equipment. *Dysdera* fangs have an enormous gape and one is plunged into the back of the woodlouse while the other pierces the belly. *D. crocata*, the commoner of our two species, is about 12 mm (½ inch) long, while *D. erythrina* does not exceed 10 mm (²/₅ inch). Only *crocata* occurs in Scotland.

Fast-running wolves

The day-shift is represented by the wolf spiders of the family Lycosidae, which you won't have any trouble in finding amongst the stones and plants of your rockery from early spring until well into the autumn. Most are rather short and dark, with relatively long hind legs. The females are especially noticeable when towing their egg-sacs behind them (see p. 139). Wolf spiders love to sunbathe on stones and plants, but they are wary creatures and scurry for safety at the slightest disturbance; even your shadow can send them running. Their large eyes are also permanently on the look-out for food, in the form of springtails and other small insects which they run down in short bursts. *Pardosa pullata*, about 6 mm ($\frac{1}{4}$ inch) long and often completely black – although the male may have a yellowish band down the middle of his body – is the commonest of several wolf spiders in our gardens. None of these small spiders has a fixed home and they bed down in any convenient spot. 'Wolf spider' is not really a good name for this group, for none can claim to be a long-distance runner and they certainly don't hunt in packs – although you might find several sunbathing together. The infamous tarantula of southern Europe is one of the larger wolf spiders. It can give a painful bite, but it's not as bad as its reputation; nor is it found in Britain.

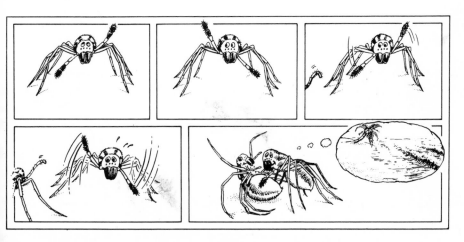

A male wolf spider signals his intentions to a female – and gets his reward.

Jumping zebras

Go to a sunny wall, preferably one clothed with lichen, and search for the aptly-named zebra spider (*Salticus scenicus*). It's about 6 mm ($\frac{1}{4}$ inch) long and clothed with flattened black and white hairs. It is one of the jumping spiders of the family Salticidae and it lives up to its name with leaps of 10 cm (4 inches) or more – but not before anchoring itself with a silken life-line which is paid out behind. The zebra spider hunts in the spring and summer sunshine, using its superb eyesight to scan the wall for any sign of movement. Your lens will reveal two huge eyes staring out from the front like a car's headlights. These eyes can move in much the same way as our own, giving the spider true binocular vision and the ability to judge distances. They can focus clearly on prey as much as 10 cm (4 inches) away, but all eight eyes can play a part in prey capture. The rear eyes pick up movement behind the spider, which immediately shuffles round for a better look. Try waving your finger behind the spider to trigger this reaction. If it decides that edible prey is in the offing, the spider walks rather jerkily towards it until it is within two or three centimetres. It then leaps forward, and within 1/20 second the victim is pinned down by the spider's sturdy front legs and the fangs are getting to work. Jumping spiders are entirely dependent on their eyes for getting food. In the dark they can literally bump into insects without recognizing them and without attempting to catch them. At sunset they retire to their silken cradles tucked under the lichens or some other protection.

Going courting

Because male spiders are generally somewhat smaller than the females, they face a few problems when they go looking for mates, and the first priority is to suppress the female's instinct to treat any small visitor as food. This is generally achieved by elaborate courtship, with each species employing its own fascinating techniques.

Males of the web-spinning species find the females' webs by scent, and they get very excited when they actually touch the web and pick up a full dose of her alluring perfume. The male then commonly starts to serenade the lady by strumming the threads of her web, and if he plays the right tune she will come over and accept him as a mate. Some theridiid and linyphiid spiders augment their web-plucking with stridulation akin to that shown by the grasshoppers and crickets; they rub one part of the body against another and produce sounds which disarm the females and allow mating to take place. The male *Meta segmentata* (see p. 124) is almost as big as the female and he can lounge around the edge of her web in comparative safety. He drives off other males, but takes no interest in the female until a fly lands in the web. Keeping the fly between himself and his intended, he holds her at bay with his extra-long front legs and 'gift-wraps' the fly with a few strands of silk. He then allows the female to approach again, gives her the fly as a present, and has his way with her as she tucks into the meal.

Hunting spiders find their mates largely by scent, but the diurnal species turn to visual signals as soon as they get close to each other. The male wolf spider waves his enlarged palps at the female and drums them audibly on the ground, sometimes to the accompaniment of a faint stridulation. The receptive female waves back with her palps and moves slowly towards the male. Excited by her approach, he speeds up his display and if she is ready to mate she reaches out to touch him with one of her front legs. The zebra spider (see p. 136) also goes in for a lot of leg-waving and actually does a jig in front of his intended. If she is impressed she simply sits still and allows him to fondle her with his front legs, after which he climbs on her back and completes the job.

Crab spiders go in for bondage. Scent and a mixture of tactile and visual signals bring the sexes into contact and the female *Xysticus cristatus* (see p. 132) then allows the male to tie her to the ground with a flimsy 'bridal veil'. She shows no inclination to escape from her bonds during mating, but has no trouble in shaking them off afterwards.

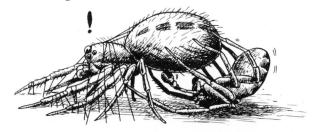

Drassodes lapidosus (see p. 133) goes in for rape. In common with other spiders, the male matures earlier than the female and goes in search of sex. He commonly takes up residence in or close to an adolescent female's retreat and waits patiently until she grows up. As soon as she has completed her final moult and acquired the necessary equipment he 'rapes' her, while she is still weak and unable to defend her virtue. Mating can also take place later, but then the male has to be very careful and he has to make many advances before she will accept him.

Making love

The spiders' sex organs open on the underside of the abdomen, but the male has none of the copulatory equipment that you might expect. Full frontal mating, facing the female's fangs, could be dangerous for the male and he uses his 'fists' instead. These are the swollen tips of his palps and, before going courting, he must charge them with sperm. Spinning a small web, he squirts his semen on to it and then sucks the fluid into his palps. Then he is ready to try his luck. Assuming he is successful in subduing the predatory instincts of his lady love, he simply pokes his palps into her body.

Several different positions may be adopted during the process, the male often riding on the female's back and reaching underneath her with his palps. Only one palp is normally used at a time, but each may be shoved in several times and the whole business can last for several hours in some species – until the palps have been squeezed dry or until the female has had enough. The female garden spider is one of the least sexy of the ladies: she has had enough after just 20 seconds, allowing the male just one quick thrust.

Divorce is immediate for most species and the male leaves to recharge his palps and search for a new mate, although he may actually court the same female all over again. It is often thought that he is eaten by the female when he has finished prodding her about, but this rarely happens – unless he is worn out from a succession of love affairs and too slow to escape. Even then he has a use, for his digested body helps to nourish the eggs which will produce his offspring.

Egg-parcels and parental care

The female spider is ready to lay her eggs a few weeks after mating, always enclosing them in silken bags of various textures. Orb-weavers generally lay in the autumn and produce fluffy egg-cocoons which they glue into bark crevices and other sheltered places – often in the mother's own retreat. *Zygiella* cocoons are commonly fixed under window sills – fluffy yellowish balls up to 10 mm (2/5 inch) across. Garden spider cocoons are similar although more common on trees and fences. The female garden spider lays up to 1,000 eggs and sheds them all in about ten minutes, but she never recovers from the effort and rarely survives more than another few weeks. Like most orb-weavers, she stays with her eggs until she dies, perhaps warding off a few parasites during her dying days, but her eggs do not hatch until the following spring.

Many hunters, including *Drassodes* and *Dysdera* and the jumping spiders, deposit their egg-cocoons in their own retreats, but the wolf spiders, most of which have no fixed home, carry their egg-bags around with them. *Pardosa pullata* and its relatives that scurry over the rockery drag their cocoons behind them, firmly attached to the spinners. If you try to remove the lentil-shaped cocoon from one of these spiders she will defend it vigorously, often digging her fangs into the tough surface fabric to get a better grip. But you *can* remove it if you are careful, and then the poor spider will spend ages hunting for it. Give it back and watch how she gleefully clasps it to her body and then re-attaches it to the spinners. In the absence of the real thing, she will even accept a small polystyrene pellet or similar objects about the size of her cocoon. When the eggs are about to hatch the spider bites through the wall of the cocoon to allow the spiderlings to escape, but they don't go far to start with – just on to mum's back, where they ride for a few days before gradually dropping off and making their own way in the world.

The nursery web spider (*Pisaura mirabilis*) is a relative of *Pardosa*, but the female carries her egg-bag in her fangs. She is commonly seen basking with it on low-growing plants in early summer. As hatching time arrives, she fixes the bag to a plant and spins a silken tent over it. She then stands guard over the tent until the babies have hatched and are ready to disperse.

To witness the ultimate in parental care you must go to a dense hedge or shrub in the summer and look for *Theridion sisyphium*, a globular black and brown spider with squiggly white lines on its abdomen. It is only about

4 mm ($^{1}/_{6}$ inch) long, but luckily it advertises its presence with an inverted thimble-like cup in the upper part of its scaffold web (see p. 130). The cup is made largely of silk, with bits of leaf and the remains of the spider's prey, and from mid-summer onwards you can find the female spider resting there with her greenish egg-bag. When the eggs hatch the mother actually feeds the youngsters with regurgitated food, and this usually takes place below the retreat with the babies scurrying up and down the scaffolding like a troupe of trapeze artistes. As they get bigger the mother introduces them to the idea of piercing prey by doing so herself and then allowing the babies to suck up the fluids that ooze out. They soon cotton on and by the time they leave home a few weeks later they are well able to deal with small prey on their own.

Growing up

Although some young spiders remain with their mothers for a while, the majority leave home very soon after hatching. Many are orphaned even before they hatch, but they instinctively know how to hunt or to make webs and, with hundreds of babies often emerging from one egg-bag, it is inevitable that some of the weaker ones fall prey to their brothers and sisters before the family breaks up. The survivors gradually disperse and the lucky ones find homes of their own. Like other arthropods, the spiders are encased in tough outer skeletons – although the abdominal skin is fairly elastic – and they have to undergo several moults as they grow (see p. 42). Moulting usually takes place in a safe retreat, although most orb-weavers moult on their webs. The process lasts anything from a few minutes to a couple of hours, depending on the size of the spider. Small species may have only five moults, while larger species may have ten, but the males always have fewer moults than the females – due to their smaller size and earlier maturity. Some males are mature several weeks before their future mates, and this gives them plenty of opportunity to size up the talent. The majority of our spiders complete their life cycles within one year.

Ballooning babies

Most of us have had small spiders land on us in the middle of nowhere and wondered where they could have come from. They have been 'ballooning' – drifting through the air on almost invisible strands of silk. This is not a

passive flight, but an active pursuit on the part of many young spiders anxious to get away from a seething mass of brothers and sisters. The youngster draws a thread from its spinners and, raising its abdomen to the sky, waits for the wind to grab the silk. Friction between silk and wind may haul out more silk, until there is enough to carry the whole spider aloft – in the same way that a kite can lift a child off its feet. Spiders lifted in this way have been caught in nets towed by aeroplanes at heights of several thousand metres. The majority perish, of course, snapped up by birds or merely landing in unsuitable places, but so great are the initial numbers that this is a very efficient way of colonizing all the suitable habitats. Many adult money spiders also take to the air in the autumn, but this is a passive flight and it occurs during sudden warm spells. Rising currents of warm air lift the spiders' drag-lines and the spiders commonly go with them.

The enemies of spiders

Clever predators they may be, but this doesn't mean that the spiders have no enemies. Birds take a good many in the garden, especially when feeding their young, and toads also enjoy them. But it is among the creepy-crawlies themselves that we find the spiders' main enemies. Ichneumons (see p. 112) of various kinds lay their eggs in the spiders' egg-bags and their grubs feed on the developing spiders. Other ichneumons lay their eggs in or on young spiders, which are then eaten alive by the ichneumon grubs. Some solitary wasps (see p. 108) specialize in collecting spiders for stocking their nests,

but the most important predators are actually other spiders. There i
usually a scrap when spiders meet, although if they are of the same specie
the fights tend to be ritualized and the weaker individual can slink away. I
is obviously not in the interests of the spiders to kill members of their ow
species. But real fights take place when spiders of different species meet, an
the weaker or less agile of the two usually ends up dead. If you confin
several spiders in one container you will eventually have just one survivor -
the 'king of the ring'. This will happen even if the spiders are all of the sam
kind, for the weaker ones cannot escape.

Much of this spider slaughter is the result of casual meetings, but ther
are some species that habitually prey on others and go out of their way t
track them down. One group, known as pirate spiders, stealthily invade th
webs of others and kill them with a bite on the leg. *Ero furcata* is th
commonest of our pirate spiders, only about 3 mm ($\frac{1}{8}$ inch) long with
mottled grey and black abdomen sometimes tinged with red. The front leg
are unusually long. You might find this pretty little spider in the webs o
small theridiid and linyphiid spiders in the garden, but it is more common i
rough grassland.

Despite their numerous enemies, spiders remain incredibly abundan
animals. Bristowe estimated that there may be more than 2,000,000 spider
in an acre of meadowland in the autumn – over 400 to the square metre
You won't find such dense populations in your garden, but there will b
plenty of spiders for you to watch and, hopefully, admire – if only for th
numbers of insect pests that they destroy.

Spidery harvestmen

The harvestmen are so named because most species mature and becom
conspicuous at about harvest-time. They are very often mistaken for spider
– a pardonable mistake because some of the long-legged species are eve
more spidery than the spiders themselves. They are often called harves
spiders but, apart from having eight legs, they have little in common wit
the true spiders. The body is just a single unit, with no obvious division, an
the second pair of legs is always the longest – something never found in th
true spiders. The eyes are also markedly different: instead of six or eigh
near the front, there are just two simple eyes perched on a little turret on th
top of the body. The animals probably have rather poor sight but, bein
largely nocturnal, this doesn't bother them and they find their way aroun
mainly by scent and touch, using the palps and the sensitive tips of th

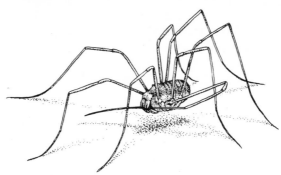

A harvestman cleaning its all-important second leg.

second pair of legs. Harvestmen can manage quite well after losing three or even four legs, but they will quickly die if they lose both of this second pair.

As far as their behaviour is concerned, the harvestmen lead very dull lives compared with the spiders. They have no silk – and therefore make no webs – no venom and no courtship. Except when washing themselves, which they do with all the grace of a ballet dancer, the harvestmen exhibit little finesse in anything. They are essentially flesh-eaters and their prey consists of a wide variety of small creatures, including spiders, centipedes and caterpillars. Food is detected by scent and then simply trampled on and pinned to the ground while the harvestman feeds. Small pincers at the front tear and crush the flesh and the harvestman sucks up the resulting fluids and small particles. Carrion is eagerly eaten, and the animals will nibble fungi and even bird droppings. They drink regularly from raindrops and dew.

The sexes are very similar, although the females of some species tend to be larger than their mates, and mating is a casual and highly promiscuous business. The only preliminary to mating is a bit of hand-holding, but this is merely to get the animals into the right face-to-face position, sometimes with their bodies slightly raised to bring their bellies closer together. The male's long, slender penis then bursts from his belly and snakes its way into the female. The animals stay together for no more than a few minutes – sometimes only seconds – and then they wander off as if nothing had happened. Each may begin a new liaison almost immediately.

About twelve species can be found roaming the garden at night or resting on the vegetation or the lower parts of walls and tree trunks by day. One of the most familiar is *Leiobunum rotundum*, which often strides into the house on its extremely long, hair-like legs. The male has an almost spherical, chestnut body only 3–4 mm (about 1/6 inch) across, while his mate is more pear-shaped and about 6 mm (¼ inch) long, with a dark mark on her back. This species is commonly found at rest on walls and tree trunks, although it is very difficult to spot. It also likes greenhouses and, like several other harvestmen, it is strongly attracted to outside toilets.

Mini-scorpions

This fearsome-looking beast almost certainly lives in your garden. But don't worry – it's only 2–3 mm (about $^1/_{10}$ inch) long and can't possibly hurt you. It's called a false scorpion but, unlike the true scorpions, it has no sting in the tail: it doesn't even have a tail. The body is grey or brown and the pincers, which may be longer than the body, are usually pale pink. Several species live in gardens, and if you want to find them you'd better have a close look at your compost heap or the leaf litter at the bottom of the hedge.

The animals prowl about in these damp places, catching mites and other tiny creatures with their pincers. The latter can inject a powerful poison, although the amount is so minute that it is effective only against the smallest animals. You can also find false scorpions in *old* birds' nests, and two species regularly live in sheds and houses, where they feed on booklice and other mini-beasts amongst old books and papers and under damp wallpaper. All are generally slow-moving, but when alarmed they will pull in their pincers and scuttle backwards with surprising speed.

Several species, especially those living in decaying matter, scatter themselves around the countryside by hitching lifts on flies, clinging tightly to the flies' hairs and dropping off wherever they fancy. Many are probably brought into the house in this way. Courtship among these tiny creatures is surprisingly elaborate and almost human; male and female take each other by the hand and dance. Only the music is missing.

Mites by the million

Mites are everywhere but, as the name suggests, they are very small and you'll see very few of the millions that inhabit your garden. The most likely to come to your notice are the bright red velvet mites that scurry over paths and walls, especially in the spring. Reaching 3–4 mm (about ¹/₆ inch) in length, they are among the largest of the mites and you can clearly see the eight legs that make them arachnids. They feed on various soil-dwelling insects and their eggs. The clover mite is another common and sometimes troublesome mite. A brownish creature just visible to the naked eye, it feeds on clovers and grasses and normally lays its eggs in bark crevices, but when trees are unavailable the mite must look elsewhere. Thousands of mites sometimes swarm up house walls in their search for egg-laying sites and they readily enter doors and windows. Densely packed and resembling a mobile patch of rust, they cause considerable alarm, although they do no damage and are easily removed by the vacuum cleaner. Such invasions are most common on new housing estates, with plenty of grass and not too many trees.

The fruit-tree red spider mite, familiar to most apple growers, is one of the few really troublesome mites in the garden. Although less than a millimetre long, it exists in immense numbers and removes so much sap from the leaves of apples and various other fruit trees that many of the leaves die. Whole trees are sometimes killed. The creature is called a spider mite because it clothes the leaves with a fine web of silk. Winter is passed in the egg stage, and when infestation is severe the twigs and branches on which the eggs are laid appear quite red. Very similar red spider mites live in greenhouses and on house plants.

If you want to see the most fascinating of your garden mites you must take a spoonful of muck from your compost heap and put it under a strong lens, or under a microscope if you can get hold of one. Bizarre 'monsters' with globular bodies will stare back and perhaps wave their spiky legs at you. These slow-moving beasties are beetle mites and there really are millions of them in your soil and compost, where they feed on fungal threads and decaying matter. Other equally spiky but faster-moving species may show their predatory natures by snatching beetle mites and sucking them dry as you watch. You might not have fairies at the bottom of your garden, but you've certainly got ogres in your compost heap.

There are also plenty of mites in the average house, although you'll need jolly good eyes to spot them. Rarely more than about a millimetre long, they occur in flour and other cereal products, amongst dried fruit, and even in ordinary household dust. Some make direct attacks on our food, while others prefer to feed on minute moulds. All flourish best in slightly damp conditions and rarely cause problems in today's heated homes. Where they do occur in any number, they can cause allergic reactions in our skin and eyes. 'Grocer's itch' was once a very common mite-induced skin irritation so called (not surprisingly) because it was especially common among grocers. Modern packaging has largely done away with the problem, for the grocer no longer has to delve into bins and sacks to weigh up dried fruit and flour or even biscuits. The best way to find some of these mites, if you feel so inclined, is to leave some cheese uncovered for a few days and then examine it closely with a good lens. Alternatively, gather some dust from a damp corner – especially from the shed or from any room that is not regularly used and heated.

Mites – a biological rag-bag

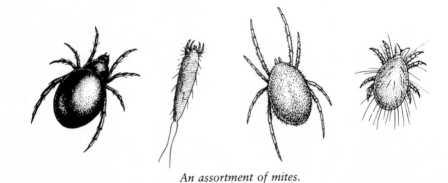

An assortment of mites.

It is impossible to define a mite in simple terms because the group is not a natural one: it is a rag-bag of several distinct lines which have little in common apart from their small size and which have been lumped together purely for convenience. The illustrations above will show you something of the immense range of form in the mites, and this is matched by an equally wide range of habits. Most mites have four pairs of legs when mature – like most other arachnids – but the early stages generally have only three pairs. The gall mites, including the one responsible for the big-bud disease of blackcurrants, have only two pairs of legs when mature.

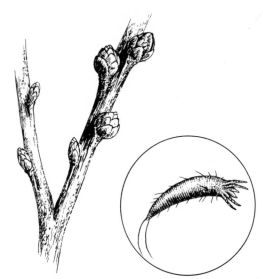

Big-bud – the excessive and abnormal growth of blackcurrant buds – is caused by a microscopic sausage-shaped mite. The mites can also transmit virus diseases to the currant bushes.

The parasitic ticks

The blood-sucking ticks are generally much bigger than the mites, but are structurally much the same and all are included in the same group, technically known as the Acarina. Ticks infest a wide range of garden birds and mammals, but you are most likely to find them on hedgehogs or on your domestic cats and dogs. There are several different species, but most of them look just like dirty grey peas, often with a tinge of deep red when they are full of blood – not a pretty sight when you find them clustered on the ears and other tender parts of the body. The beasts take about three years to grow up, during which time they take just three meals – one meal a year, usually in the spring. Each meal lasts several days,

and the tick's body swells visibly as it feeds. Between meals the ticks rest on the ground, usually concealed in turf or moss, and when ready for a refill they crawl up the grass blades and wait to climb aboard any passing animal. Your pets can thus very easily acquire ticks in the hedgerow or in the surrounding grassland. They don't get them, as many people believe, just by coming into contact with hedgehogs. You can acquire your own ticks by walking through infested grassland in late spring and, as I know from personal experience, they are most likely to plug in if you sit down for a picnic. The sheep tick is the usual culprit in such places.

If you have to remove ticks, from yourself or from your animals, don't be tempted to yank them out by brute force. Their mouthparts are plugged very firmly into the flesh and yanking on the body generally leaves the mouthparts behind, often leading to unpleasant sores. Smear the ticks with methylated spirit or some similar solvent to make them release their hold before you pick them off. Touching them with a lighted cigarette or some other hot object has the same effect, but needs a steady hand.

A blood-filled tick nestling in its host's fur.

Scorpions in the wall

I can't imagine many gardeners enthusing over the idea of scorpions lurking in their walls, but if you're lucky enough to have a garden in southern Europe you'll probably harbour quite a few of these curious creatures. By far the commonest is Euscorpius flavicaudis, *a small dark brown creature with a yellow tip to its curved tail. Luckily, it's harmless, and is unwilling to use the sting in its tail even when provoked – but this is certainly not true of many other scorpions, so it's not sensible to experiment. The scorpion generally hides by day, although I have seen it crawling over shady walls in many Mediterranean* towns in the daytime. At night, it comes out to hunt, but you are more likely to find it resting in a crevice with its pincers jutting out and ready to grab any passing insect or other small creature. In favourable localities you can find several of them on a square metre of wall. You're not likely to find these little creatures in British gardens, although they do arrive on ships from time to time and the species has been established around a Kent dockyard for over 100 years. It also occurs in several goods yards in southern England and could eventually establish itself in our gardens.

FOURTEEN LEGS:
WOODLICE . . . OR SOWBUGS
. . . OR TIGGY-HOGS

It seems unlikely that any of our animals has more local names than the woodlouse. Writing in 1935, Dr Walter Collinge, Keeper of the Yorkshire Museum at York, listed 65 regional names for these fascinating creatures. Many of these names are no longer used, but you can still find 'bibble-bugs' in Staffordshire, 'gammer-sows' in Wales, 'coffin-cutters' in Ireland and 'cudworms' in Shropshire. This latter name stems from the practice of dosing cattle with woodlice to improve their cud-chewing. The idea of woodlice scuttling around inside the rumen and encouraging the cow to regurgitate its food sounds plausible, although tough on the woodlice, but the practice was based more on the resemblance of the rolled-up woodlouse to a medicinal pill. Pill-bug is, of course, a widespread name for those species that can roll into a ball, for these were once thought to have considerable medicinal value. They were given to people until not so long ago. In 1833 one W.G. Black wrote of a Penzance woman who prescribed woodlice to be swallowed as pills for scrofula (tuberculosis). The patients had to gather their own 'pills', and the wise woman of Penzance actually reared them in a corner of her garden. We're not told how much she charged! I doubt if the poor woodlice had any beneficial effect on either cows or people.

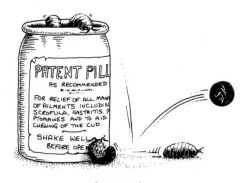

Many local names include the words 'hog' and 'pig', possibly referring to the scavenging habits of the woodlouse. The Lancashire name of 'fairies' pigs' conjures up a fascinating picture of what might go on at the bottom of the garden, while the Devon name of 'God's pigs' suggests a link with old church buildings rather than a direct connection with religion. Woodlice thrive in damp places and, until quite recently when churches have got warmer, would have found most churches much to their liking. The regular occurrence of woodlice in the house suggests a certain amount of dampness, and this may be the basis of the old idea that the animals are unlucky in the house.

So what are these little creepy-crawlies that have received so many popular or folk names? They've got too many legs for insects or spiders, and not enough to be centipedes or millipedes. They belong to another group of arthropods called crustaceans. They are distant cousins of the crabs and lobsters that have managed to invade the land, although they have not yet completely shaken off their aquatic ancestry. They still need to live in damp places, and they are generally active only at night, when the air is cool and damp. Most of them can breathe only when their bodies are covered with a film of water.

Rarely more than about 20 mm ($^4/5$ inch) long, our garden woodlice are generally grey or brown and their bodies are covered with overlapping horny plates. The latter are impregnated to a greater or lesser extent with lime, but they lack a waterproof covering such as we find in the insects and the woodlice can't survive for long in dry air because they lose too much water. Underneath the body there are seven pairs of walking legs and towards the back, five pairs of 'breathing legs'. Each breathing leg consists of two leaf-like flaps, the inner one of which is extremely thin and well supplied with blood. As long as it is covered by a film of water it acts just like a fish's gill: oxygen dissolves in the film of water and then passes through the tissues and into the bloodstream. The outer flaps protect the inner ones, but in some woodlice they are beginning to play a role in breathing themselves. Some of the outer flaps are permeated by minute branching tubes which open to the air through a tiny pore. Air can pass into the tubes, and oxygen can pass from them into the blood system. This is, of course, a very simple version of the breathing tubes or tracheae found in the insects, and one day the woodlice may be able to breathe without the need for a film of water around them. They will, of course, have to develop waterproof coats before they can really invade dry habitats, but already those with simple breathing tubes can survive in drier places than those without. The tubes, known as pseudotracheae, can be seen as white patches on the underside of the rear half of the body.

The rear end bears a pair of forked limbs known as uropods, which usually stick out beyond the body and have a sensory function just like the hind legs of the centipede (see p. 163). The outer branch, which is generally much stouter than the inner one, also secretes repellent fluids which protect the woodlouse from various predators.

The common pill-bug – more strongly domed than its fellow woodlice.

Not all woodlice can roll into a ball. The only common garden species to do this is *Armadillidium vulgare* – the 'common little armadillo' in English – which is one of the unfortunate pill-bugs referred to on p. 149. It is steely grey and more strongly domed than most woodlice, and its uropods do not stick out from the rear end. It can stand drier conditions than most woodlice as a result of its ability to roll up and reduce evaporation from its surface, and also because it has a thicker coat and much better developed breathing tubes than most woodlice. The ability to roll up also gives the animal some protection from predators, especially the smaller ones that cannot get their teeth or fangs into the hard ball. Look for the pill-bug along the base of the garden wall, where the mortar provides the lime needed for the thick coat. When rolled up, the animal can be distinguished from the pill millipede (see p. 160) by its colour and also by the numerous small plates of the tail end, which remain visible at all times.

A rotten diet

Woodlice feed mainly at night, searching for goodies on the ground and on walls and tree trunks. Their main food consists of dead and decaying plant matter, including rotting wood, but living plants are not ignored. Seedlings are commonly nibbled – the only real damage done by woodlice – and *Armadillidium* will occasionally nibble a small area of lawn for you. Fungi are sometimes eaten, while the powdery green algae on walls and tree trunks are staple foods for woodlice with a climbing bent. Dung and carrion are occasionally sampled, especially the dung of herbivorous mammals which is rich in plant remains. By eating decaying matter, the animals speed up the return of minerals to the soil, but this is a two-stage process. The first stage may be little more than a fragmentation of the dead leaves and other materials, with as much as 90 per cent of the ingested matter passing out virtually unchanged in the animals' droppings. The fragmented materials are then more easily broken down by bacteria, and the woodlice return to eat their own droppings, which this time give up much more of their nutrient material, including copper compounds vital for the formation of the animals' blood pigments.

The animals' activity is controlled mainly by humidity and light. On dry nights, when they lose water rapidly, they stay out for much shorter periods than they do on damp nights, and they don't climb so high on walls and tree trunks. They are also less inclined to climb high on moonlit nights, but it is not easy to distinguish the effects of light and humidity here because moonlit nights are usually associated with low humidity. As dawn breaks, or long before on a dry night, the woodlice head for shelter again, but they don't necessarily use the same bed every day. When the animals begin to feel dry, or when they are exposed to light, they scurry about quite quickly, but when they meet damper or darker conditions they slow down and start to turn this way and that. The damper it gets, the slower they get, and eventually they stop altogether – a neat bit of behaviour designed to ensure that the animals always come to rest in a suitable dark, damp crevice. There

is also a chemical attraction between individuals of the same species, often drawing hundreds of individuals together in one resting place – under a single log or piece of loose bark, for example. Such a resting place would acquire the animals' scent, and would then draw them back each day.

An internal clock, based on the length of day, wakes the woodlice in the evening, but why, if they're so addicted to damp places, do they bother to get up and wander about? Their sleeping quarters are generally surrounded by plenty of rotting plant material, so it can't be hunger that drives them out. Water again seems to be the answer – too much of it this time. Just as the woodlice can lose water through their skins, so they can absorb it, and after several hours in their soggy beds they just have to get up and go for a walk to get rid of the excess water.

Babies in pouches

Male and female woodlice look alike, unless you turn them over to look for the male's copulatory equipment. This consists of a pair of slender stylets springing from his second pair of 'breathing legs' and surrounding his genital opening. Mating takes place in the dark and has seldom been witnessed, but it seems to be a rather casual affair with little courtship. The male is attracted to the female by scent, and if she stays still he climbs on top of her and starts to kiss the back of her head. He then slips his rear end underneath her and pokes her with his sperm-laden stylets.

The female is not ready to mate, however, until she has prepared her brood pouch, which develops under the front half of her body. It is formed by a number of horny plates which grow in from her sides and meet in the mid-line. The pouch fills with liquid and the fertilized eggs are passed into

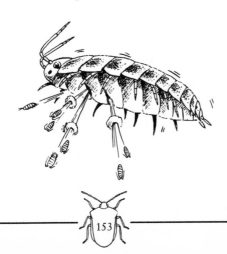

it. They hatch after about a month, although the time varies with the different species, and the liquid gradually disappears, leaving the baby woodlice crawling around in the pouch. They remain there for a few days, during which time they get darker in colour and become more and more active. They gradually find their way out through gaps between the plates. Although there may be as many as 250 eggs in some species, they don't all survive and only twenty or thirty youngsters may make it to the outside world. They start to breed when they are about two years old, if they escape their numerous enemies, and they may survive for about four years altogether.

Strip shows

Like all the arthropods (see p. 42), the woodlice have to change their skins periodically as they grow up, but instead of stripping off all at once, they do it in two stages. The rear half of the outer skeleton is lost first, and if discovered at this stage – by lifting up a log, for example – the animal looks very odd: the front half is the normal greyish colour, while the rear is creamy white. The rear end soon hardens and darkens, however, and then the old front skin is shed, leaving the animal with a pale front end for a few days. The woodlice don't wander about like this, however, for it would be dangerous – and, indeed, very difficult – to move about before the new coat has hardened.

CORd... SHE'S HALF NAKED... ...HMMM....

Woodlouse enemies

Despite the repellent secretions of their uropods (see p. 151) and other parts of their bodies, the woodlice have numerous enemies, including various backboned animals as well as other creepy-crawlies. Shrews are the main

154

vertebrate predators of garden woodlice, although toads will also eat a fair number when they find them. Hedgehogs eat surprisingly few, as far as we can tell by examining their droppings. Invertebrate predators include ground beetles, centipedes, harvestmen and various spiders, including wolf spiders and the specialist woodlouse hunter *Dysdera* (see p. 134). There are also a number of flies, related to the bluebottles, that parasitize woodlice in much the same way that the ichneumons (see p. 112) attack other insects. If you keep woodlice in captivity, which is an easy and interesting way to learn something of their habits, you may well disover some of these parasites emerging from your charges.

The gardener and housewife destroy many woodlice around the house and garden in the belief that they are harmful, but the animals probably do more good than harm and, although they might occasionally need controlling in the greenhouse, they can safely be left alone to get on with their scavenging ways.

Some garden woodlice

Species	Antenna	Colour	Habitat
Porcellio scaber	2 small segments	Usually dull grey and pimply.	Relatively dry parts, including rubbish heaps: the only one common on walls and tree trunks.
Oniscus asellus	3 small segments	Brownish grey with paler spots: flatter and more shiny than *Porcellio.*	Damper parts: under logs and stones and in damper parts of compost heap.
Philoscia muscorum	As *Oniscus*	Mottled brown or red with a dark line down the centre.	Grass and other dense vegetation: runs rapidly when disturbed.
Armadillidium vulgare	As *Porcellio*	Steely grey: strongly domed.	Relatively dry, grassy places: rolls into a ball when disturbed.

There are nearly 50 different kinds of woodlice living in the British Isles, although not all are natives and only about half a dozen turn up with any regularity in the garden. Some are very small, and rarely seen unless you take a magnifying glass to the compost heap, while others literally can't be missed. The common species are quite easy to identify by shape and colour and by the form of the antennae, as shown on the chart on the preceding page. All are found mainly in the less disturbed parts of the garden and I doubt if there is any garden without at least one of the species, even if it has to live in flower pots on the patio.

LOTS AND LOTS OF LEGS: THE MILLIPEDES AND CENTIPEDES

Millipedes and centipedes are essentially nocturnal animals, but they're easy enough to find under logs and stones in the garden. Like the woodlice, they lack waterproof coats and have to stay in damp spots by day. They soon scurry for fresh cover when you expose them to the light. An inborn tendency to move away from light and away from a dry atmosphere ensures that they eventually end up in safe places. Millipedes and centipedes all have many body segments and many pairs of legs and they are commonly lumped together as myriapods, a name meaning 'many feet': but the two groups are not closely related.

Millipedes are slow-moving herbivores and scavengers, while the centipedes are relatively speedy predators. Structurally, they are easily distinguished by looking at the legs: millipedes have two pairs of legs on most segments, while the centipedes have only one pair per segment. In addition, the millipede body is normally circular in cross-section and the centipede body is clearly flattened from top to bottom. Centipedes are nearly all yellow or brown, but our garden millipedes are often black.

1,000 feet – never!

The name millipede literally means 1,000 feet, but not even the large tropical species have quite that number. The British species are veritable tiddlers in the group and rarely have more than about 200 feet. Many of our species have less than 100 feet, but they can still generate quite a push: hold a millipede in a clenched fist and you'll be surprised at the force with which it probes between your fingers. This is, of course, how the animal makes its way through the soil and leaf litter in which it lives. Controlling scores of legs poses no problem for the millipedes and they never seem to trip over their own feet – although they don't move very quickly. Our fastest species trundle along at all of a metre per minute and never seem to get out of first gear: the little legs move quite quickly, but the body won't be hurried.

If you can persuade a millipede to walk over a flat surface you will see the

legs moving in groups. The hind legs are the first to move forward, and then each of the other legs moves fractionally after the one behind it, causing a ripple or wave to move forward along the body. By the time this wave has travelled a short way forward, the rear legs are already on the backstroke and about to start a new wave. Several such waves can be seen passing forward along the body at any one time, propelling the millipede smoothly and slowly forward.

Most millipedes live in the soil or leaf litter, where it is permanently dark and damp, but even here they tend to be nocturnal. It is thought that they have in-built alarm clocks which wake them up when the temperature falls in the evening. Even a very small drop in temperature is sufficient to wake them. The animals are most numerous, in terms of species as well as individuals, in chalky soils, which provide an abundance of the calcium salts needed to strengthen the animals' outer coats. Millipedes are basically scavengers, feeding on all kinds of dead and decaying vegetable matter and also taking small amounts of carrion such as dead worms and slugs. Seedling plants may be nibbled, but the animals' jaws are weak and they cannot chomp their way through anything tough. They are commonly accused of damaging potatoes and other crops, and certainly do hollow out the occasional root or potato tuber, but they are not strong enough to penetrate a sound one. They wait for other creatures to make the initial breakthrough and then move in, attracted by the sugary sap oozing from the wound. Damage is most serious in dry weather and it seems likely that the millipedes are more interested in moisture than food when they attack crops.

About fifty kinds of millipede occur in Britain, and the three main groups – known as snake, pill and flat-backed millipedes – are shown in the accompanying chart.

THE MANY-LEGGED MINI-BEASTS' WHO'S WHO

SNAKE MILLIPEDES: circular in cross section and often shiny black.
Natural history: the body is coiled into a flat spiral at rest, and many species adopt the same posture when alarmed. Most species feed at or below ground level, often at considerable depths, although some climb plants in damp weather to nibble fruit – especially raspberries. Several can be found resting under loose bark by day. More than half of the British millipedes belong to this group.

PILL MILLIPEDES: strongly domed and usually grey or black.
Natural history: the body is short and fat and just like a woodlouse – until you count the legs: there are far more than the 7 pairs found in woodlice. The body can be rolled into a ball, with the head completely protected by the broad shield at the hind end. Rolling up gives some protection from desiccation as well as from enemies and pill millipedes can live in drier places than other kinds. Look for them at the base of a wall or hedge.

FLAT-BACKED MILLIPEDES: 19 or 20 body segments. The body is basically cylindrical, but broad flanges extending from the top of each segment give it a flat-topped appearance – rather like centipedes, although with more legs.
Natural history: flat-backs live mainly in leaf litter and compost.

SOIL-LOVING CENTIPEDES: at least 37 pairs of legs.
Natural history: very slender centipedes, spending almost all of their lives in the soil. This group contains about half of the British species.

STONE-DWELLING CENTIPEDES: 15 pairs of legs when mature.
Natural history: fast running, shiny brown centipedes, most likely to be found lurking under stones.

Poisonous protection

Most millipedes have poison glands on the sides of the body. The red spots of the spotted snake millipede (*Blaniulus guttulatus*) – a common pest of potatoes in the garden – are the glands showing through the pale body and not simply decorations. When the animals are alarmed, the glands secrete their nauseous fluids, containing such unpleasant substances as chlorine, iodine and even cyanide. Pick up a millipede and you'll often find that the fluids stain your fingers, although our British species do not secrete enough to harm you – unlike some of those from warmer countries. The fluids repel most of the millipedes' enemies, but do not offer complete protection. Toads and hedgehogs mop up millipedes quite happily, and the starling is not averse to a millipede meal either. The poisons are best developed in the snake millipedes. Flat-backs don't exude visible amounts of fluid, but if you confine several of them in a small jar for a while you might be able to detect a faint smell of almonds (cyanide). The pill millipedes rely on their ability to roll up for protection and have no repellent glands.

A pill millipede, distinguished from a pill woodlouse (p. 151) *by the broad shield at the rear end.*

A leggy embrace

In contrast to the centipedes (see p. 167), the millipedes make quite a thing of their sex lives, although few people have ever seen their amorous antics. You've probably never even thought of millipedes – or any other creepy-crawly – getting sexy, but the millipedes have been going in for cuddling for millions of years – and with so many legs at their disposal it's quite a performance. Of course, it's all designed to get the right bits into the right place, but the preliminaries might be just as much fun for the millipedes as they are for humans.

The millipedes' genital openings are on or just behind the 2nd pair of legs,

but most male millipedes actually use one or both pairs of legs on the 7th segment to transfer sperm to the females. These legs are called gonopods and are distinctively shaped; you'll have to examine them under a microscope for accurate identification of some species. During mating, the front halves of the two lovers are locked face to face in a many-legged embrace that may last for several hours. The male's gonopods become lined up with the female's genital openings, but before he can deliver his sperm he must charge up his gonopods, which he does by flexing his body to bring the gonopods up to his own genital openings.

Pill millipedes mate in a head-to-tail position, for in this group the male's hind legs are modified to form the gonopods.

After mating the female millipede generally builds a simple nest for her eggs. Designs differ slightly, but the nests are usually dome-shaped chambers made from the females' excrement and attached to stones or other solid objects in the soil. The circumference of the nest is roughly equal to the length of the female's body. Female flat-backs generally coil around their nests and remain on guard for a week or so. Pill millipedes make no nests, merely covering each egg with excrement and abandoning it in the soil.

Young millipedes emerge from the eggs with just three pairs of legs and could well be mistaken for insects at this stage, but they don't remain like this for long. Within hours the little millipedes undergo a moult and acquire four more pairs of legs. During the next few months they pass through another six moults, gaining more segments and legs each time until they reach the adult stage. Moulting is a dangerous business, as it is for any arthropod, because the animal is immobile and defenceless until its new

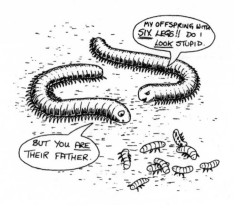

coat has hardened (see p. 42). Millipedes minimize the dangers by building moulting chambers, similar to their nests, and remaining there, out of the way of predators and parasites, until the moult is complete. Pill millipedes build no such chambers, however, and take their chances naked in the leaf litter.

100 feet – sometimes!

The speed of centipedes – most obvious as they scurry away from disturbance – rightly suggests that they are predatory creatures and is at least partly responsible for the widespread fear of these interesting animals. But speed is deceptive and the centipedes are generally speedy only in relation to their own body size. Our garden centipedes might belt along at speeds of 5 metres per minute (less than ·2 m.p.h.) when alarmed, but they keep this up for no more than a couple of seconds even if they don't find a refuge, appearing to

tire quickly and slowing down to a sedate metre per second or even less. They then look much more friendly, but there is no need to fear any British centipede, whatever its speed – unless you are another small invertebrate.

The name centipede literally means 100 feet, but none has exactly this number. Some have considerably more and many have considerably less, with our most familiar garden species having just 15 pairs of legs when mature. There is always an odd number of pairs, one pair belonging to each segment of the body. The last pair of legs is longer than the others and, with a good supply of sense organs, they act as an extra pair of antennae – very useful for animals which often have to move backwards in narrow crevices or in tunnels in the soil. The true antennae, springing from the front of the head, resemble strings of beads and may be as much as half the length of the body. They are loaded with sense organs which help the centipede to smell and feel its way around. Sight is generally very poor, and many centipedes have no eyes at all, although the general body surface is sufficiently sensitive to light for the animals to know when they've been uncovered and to act accordingly.

Almost any other creepy-crawly is fair game for the centipede. Even armoured beetles and relatively large worms and slugs are subdued by the centipede's fangs and poison, but few millipedes seem to be eaten – presumably because of their repellent secretions. The fangs curve around

the head and are clearly visible if you can persuade a centipede to sit still for a few seconds. Better still, hold a specimen in your fingers and watch the fangs trying to bite. Some of our larger British centipedes can pierce human skin and produce a short-lived stinging sensation, but they don't inject enough venom to do you any real harm and they won't even attack if you don't molest them. I wouldn't advise picking up the large and colourful *Scolopendra cingulatus* which can be found lurking under stones in southern Europe, for this does bite when molested and can cause prolonged and severe discomfort. Some of its tropical relatives are as much as 30 mm (12 inches) long and it's certainly not a good idea to tangle with these – although very few people would ever get a chance, for these big centipedes can run pretty fast.

The enemies of centipedes include birds, shrews and toads. Ground beetles and hunting spiders also take plenty of small centipedes, but a centipede's worst enemy is another centipede, for the animals are more than willing to indulge in a bit of cannibalism.

Soil lovers

Less than fifty species of centipede live in Britain, and half of these belong to the group known as geophilomorphs – soil lovers in English, although some species prefer the seashore to the garden. They are long and thread-like and often called wireworms, although this name really belongs to the larvae of certain click beetles (see p. 93). They have at least 37 pairs of legs, but these are relatively short and the animals are rather slow-moving for centipedes – both features being associated with a life spent almost entirely in the soil.

The animals also lack eyes. These are the centipedes that you are most likely to find while digging your garden. The commonest species has the tongue-twisting name *Necrophloeophagus longicornis*. It is yellow with a rather long brick-red head and a distinct almond smell when handled. Although up to 45 mm (2 inches) long, it is a mere 1 mm broad.

One of the most striking things about these soil-dwelling centipedes is their amazing flexibility – easily seen if you put one in a confined space. The animal can double back on itself with ease and can even fold itself up like a tiny hank of rope. The secret lies in the large number of body joints. There is, of course, a movable joint between each segment, but this is only half the story. The skeletal plates covering the top and bottom of each segment are themselves divided into two and, although there is only limited movement between the two sections, the arrangement effectively doubles the number of body joints and the flexibility of the body as a whole. Being a contortionist is clearly a valuable asset in the soil, where the animal has to manoeuvre in confined spaces and often comes to a dead end against a stone, but even then some tunnels are too narrow for turning and the centipedes have to engage reverse gear. Aided by the sensitive hind legs, many can travel backwards almost as efficiently as they move forwards.

Stone dwellers

Technically known as lithobiomorphs, the stone dwellers are the familiar shiny reddish brown centipedes that scurry away when we lift logs and stones. They are broader and less flexible than the soil-dwelling species and, with much longer legs, less suited to burrowing – although they may go down into the soil in very cold or very dry weather. They feed on the ground at night and return to their shelters before daybreak, almost always coming to rest in crevices where both upper and lower body surfaces are in contact with something. Many find both food and shelter in the garden compost heap.

Adults have 15 pairs of legs, each pair being longer than the pair in front – an arrangement that enables the animals to run rapidly with long strides but without each pair of legs treading on the toes of the pair in front. The head bears a number of simple eyes, but these are unlikely to be much use in finding food and the animals rely mainly on smell and touch. In addition to the sense organs on their antennae, they have numerous sensory bristles scattered all over the legs and body and these undoubtedly help the centipedes to detect the movements of potential prey. *Lithobius forficatus*,

A typical stone dweller.

up to 30 mm (1¹/₅ inches) long and 4 mm (¹/₆ inch) broad, is the commonest of several very similar species.

The fastest centipede

Scutigera coleoptrata, *otherwise known as the house centipede, can hardly claim to be a creepy-crawly, for this leggy creature has been timed at 50 cm per second (about 1¹/₆ m.p.h.) and in warm weather it can keep this up for several metres. It is a native of southern Europe, where it hunts on old walls at night. Unlike the other centipedes, it has efficient compound eyes like those of the insects (see p. 47) and it hunts by sight. Flies, moths and other insects are its main prey. By day the animal hides in a crevice. It is well established in the Channel Islands, where it is often found in greenhouses, and occasionally arrives in Britain as a stowaway amongst imported fruit and vegetables. It establishes itself temporarily in houses and other buildings, but you are unlikely to see it roaming the garden.*

Long-distance love affair

We know very little about the sex life of centipedes, but what little we do know suggests that they don't have much of a love life at all. The sexes are generally very similar and they have none of the expected copulatory equipment. None of the few species studied goes in for sex in the normal way. It's all done with scent. In the presence of a mature female, the male spins a small silken web and deposits a small packet of sperm on it. The female then ambles over to the web and picks up the packet, known as a spermatophore, with a small pair of claspers at her hind end. That seems to be the extent of the centipedes' love life. 'Excitement' over, the female gradually absorbs the sperm into her body. You can find females carrying the milky white sperm packets at any time from spring to autumn. Spring and summer 'matings' are soon followed by egg-laying, but autumn impregnations do not bear fruit until the following spring.

The lithobiomorph females merely scatter their eggs in the earth, after coating them with mucus and soil particles for protection, but the other garden centipedes lay batches of eggs in small chambers in the soil and coil around them until they have hatched and the babies are able to fend for themselves. If the female is separated from her eggs the latter usually develop moulds and fail to hatch, and it seems likely that the female keeps the moulds at bay by continually licking her eggs. Under normal circumstances the eggs hatch within a few weeks. Lithobiomorph youngsters have only six pairs of legs on hatching, but they are fully active right from the start. They acquire further legs at each moult until they are fully equipped. Youngsters of the other centipede groups have the full complement of legs when they hatch, but neither the legs nor the fangs are properly developed at this stage and the babies have to undergo two moults before they are ready to leave the protection of the nest. Centipedes take up to three years to mature, and if they manage to escape their numerous enemies they may live for about six years.

Their predatory nature means that the centipedes should be welcome in the garden, for they undoubtedly destroy a goodly number of soil-dwelling pests and only very occasionally nibble plant roots – usually in drought conditions when they get rather thirsty. The soil-dwelling species are not large enough or numerous enough to have any significant effect on the aeration and drainage of the soil.

TAIL-PIECE: ENJOY YOUR GARDEN GUESTS

If I have shown in the preceding pages that garden creepy-crawlies are not all villains, I have achieved part of my aim in writing this book. If I have shown that they lead interesting lives I shall be happy. And if I have encouraged you to tolerate them and perhaps even welcome them into your garden the creepy-crawlies will be happy. But don't leave it there: take a break in your garden and lean on your spade or sit in your deckchair and watch. There is still a great deal to be learned about the inter-relationships of even our commonest garden guests, and the amateur naturalist can contribute a great deal in this sphere just by simple observation. The more we learn about the creepy-crawlies and the larger animals that visit or reside in our gardens, the easier it will be to strike that all-important equilibrium between productive gardening and wildlife gardening – an equilibrium with the garden's guests keeping each other in check and protecting our cultivated plants without the use of harmful poisons. This achieved, the garden really can be a haven for wildlife as well as providing food for the family. You'll enjoy your garden even more.

FURTHER READING

R. Blackman, *Aphids* (Ginn & Co., 1974)

W.S. Bristowe, *The World of Spiders* (Collins, 1958)

*D.J. Carter & B. Hargreaves, *A Field Guide to Caterpillars of Butterflies and Moths in Britain and Europe* (Collins, 1986)

*M. Chinery, *Collins Guide to the Insects of Britain and Western Europe* (Collins, 1986)

M. Chinery, *The Natural History of the Garden* (Collins, 1977)

M. Chinery, *The Living Garden* (Dorling Kindersley, 1986)

*D. Jones, *The Country Life Guide to Spiders of Britain and Northern Europe* (Country Life, 1983)

*M.P. Kerney & R.A.D. Cameron, *A Field Guide to the Land Snails of Britain and North-West Europe* (Collins, 1979)

*H. Mourier, O. Winding & E. Sunesen, *Collins Guide to Wildlife in House and Home* (Collins, 1977)

*D. Nichols, J. Cooke & D. Whiteley, *The Oxford Book of Invertebrates* (Oxford University Press, 1971)

J. Owen, *Garden Life* (Chatto & Windus, 1983)

N.W. Runham & P.J. Hunter, *Terrestrial Slugs* (Hutchinson University Library, 1970)

T.H. Savory, *The Spider's Web* (Warne, 1952)

*A.E. Stubbs & S.J. Falk, *British Hoverflies* (British Entomological & Natural History Society, 1983)

S.L. Sutton, *Woodlice* (Ginn and Co., 1972)

M. Tweedie, *Pleasure from Insects* (David and Charles, 1968)

P. Whalley, *Butterfly Watching* (Severn House, 1980)

* Titles marked with an asterisk are primarily for the identification of animals.

INDEX